Mometrix
TEST PREPARATION

Virginia
SOL Chemistry
Secrets Study Guide

DEAR FUTURE EXAM SUCCESS STORY

First of all, **THANK YOU** for purchasing Mometrix study materials!

Second, congratulations! You are one of the few determined test-takers who are committed to doing whatever it takes to excel on your exam. **You have come to the right place.** We developed these study materials with one goal in mind: to deliver you the information you need in a format that's concise and easy to use.

In addition to optimizing your guide for the content of the test, we've outlined our recommended steps for breaking down the preparation process into small, attainable goals so you can make sure you stay on track.

We've also analyzed the entire test-taking process, identifying the most common pitfalls and showing how you can overcome them and be ready for any curveball the test throws you.

Standardized testing is one of the biggest obstacles on your road to success, which only increases the importance of doing well in the high-pressure, high-stakes environment of test day. Your results on this test could have a significant impact on your future, and this guide provides the information and practical advice to help you achieve your full potential on test day.

Your success is our success

We would love to hear from you! If you would like to share the story of your exam success or if you have any questions or comments in regard to our products, please contact us at **800-673-8175** or **support@mometrix.com**.

Thanks again for your business and we wish you continued success!

Sincerely,
The Mometrix Test Preparation Team

Need more help? Check out our flashcards at:
http://MometrixFlashcards.com/SOL

Written and edited by the Mometrix Exam Secrets Test Prep Team
Printed in the United States of America

TABLE OF CONTENTS

Introduction

Thank you for purchasing this resource! You have made the choice to prepare yourself for a test that could have a huge impact on your future, and this guide is designed to help you be fully ready for test day. Obviously, it's important to have a solid understanding of the test material, but you also need to be prepared for the unique environment and stressors of the test, so that you can perform to the best of your abilities.

For this purpose, the first section that appears in this guide is the **Secret Keys**. We've devoted countless hours to meticulously researching what works and what doesn't, and we've boiled down our findings to the five most impactful steps you can take to improve your performance on the test. We start at the beginning with study planning and move through the preparation process, all the way to the testing strategies that will help you get the most out of what you know when you're finally sitting in front of the test.

We recommend that you start preparing for your test as far in advance as possible. However, if you've bought this guide as a last-minute study resource and only have a few days before your test, we recommend that you skip over the first two Secret Keys since they address a long-term study plan.

If you struggle with **test anxiety**, we strongly encourage you to check out our recommendations for how you can overcome it. Test anxiety is a formidable foe, but it can be beaten, and we want to make sure you have the tools you need to defeat it.

Secret Key #1 – Plan Big, Study Small

There's a lot riding on your performance. If you want to ace this test, you're going to need to keep your skills sharp and the material fresh in your mind. You need a plan that lets you review everything you need to know while still fitting in your schedule. We'll break this strategy down into three categories.

Information Organization

Start with the information you already have: the official test outline. From this, you can make a complete list of all the concepts you need to cover before the test. Organize these concepts into groups that can be studied together, and create a list of any related vocabulary you need to learn so you can brush up on any difficult terms. You'll want to keep this vocabulary list handy once you actually start studying since you may need to add to it along the way.

Time Management

Once you have your set of study concepts, decide how to spread them out over the time you have left before the test. Break your study plan into small, clear goals so you have a manageable task for each day and know exactly what you're doing. Then just focus on one small step at a time. When you manage your time this way, you don't need to spend hours at a time studying. Studying a small block of content for a short period each day helps you retain information better and avoid stressing over how much you have left to do. You can relax knowing that you have a plan to cover everything in time. In order for this strategy to be effective though, you have to start studying early and stick to your schedule. Avoid the exhaustion and futility that comes from last-minute cramming!

Study Environment

The environment you study in has a big impact on your learning. Studying in a coffee shop, while probably more enjoyable, is not likely to be as fruitful as studying in a quiet room. It's important to keep distractions to a minimum. You're only planning to study for a short block of time, so make the most of it. Don't pause to check your phone or get up to find a snack. It's also important to **avoid multitasking**. Research has consistently shown that multitasking will make your studying dramatically less effective. Your study area should also be comfortable and well-lit so you don't have the distraction of straining your eyes or sitting on an uncomfortable chair.

The time of day you study is also important. You want to be rested and alert. Don't wait until just before bedtime. Study when you'll be most likely to comprehend and remember. Even better, if you know what time of day your test will be, set that time aside for study. That way your brain will be used to working on that subject at that specific time and you'll have a better chance of recalling information.

Finally, it can be helpful to team up with others who are studying for the same test. Your actual studying should be done in as isolated an environment as possible, but the work of organizing the information and setting up the study plan can be divided up. In between study sessions, you can discuss with your teammates the concepts that you're all studying and quiz each other on the details. Just be sure that your teammates are as serious about the test as you are. If you find that your study time is being replaced with social time, you might need to find a new team.

Secret Key #2 – Make Your Studying Count

You're devoting a lot of time and effort to preparing for this test, so you want to be absolutely certain it will pay off. This means doing more than just reading the content and hoping you can remember it on test day. It's important to make every minute of study count. There are two main areas you can focus on to make your studying count.

Retention

It doesn't matter how much time you study if you can't remember the material. You need to make sure you are retaining the concepts. To check your retention of the information you're learning, try recalling it at later times with minimal prompting. Try carrying around flashcards and glance at one or two from time to time or ask a friend who's also studying for the test to quiz you.

To enhance your retention, look for ways to put the information into practice so that you can apply it rather than simply recalling it. If you're using the information in practical ways, it will be much easier to remember. Similarly, it helps to solidify a concept in your mind if you're not only reading it to yourself but also explaining it to someone else. Ask a friend to let you teach them about a concept you're a little shaky on (or speak aloud to an imaginary audience if necessary). As you try to summarize, define, give examples, and answer your friend's questions, you'll understand the concepts better and they will stay with you longer. Finally, step back for a big picture view and ask yourself how each piece of information fits with the whole subject. When you link the different concepts together and see them working together as a whole, it's easier to remember the individual components.

Finally, practice showing your work on any multi-step problems, even if you're just studying. Writing out each step you take to solve a problem will help solidify the process in your mind, and you'll be more likely to remember it during the test.

Modality

Modality simply refers to the means or method by which you study. Choosing a study modality that fits your own individual learning style is crucial. No two people learn best in exactly the same way, so it's important to know your strengths and use them to your advantage.

For example, if you learn best by visualization, focus on visualizing a concept in your mind and draw an image or a diagram. Try color-coding your notes, illustrating them, or creating symbols that will trigger your mind to recall a learned concept. If you learn best by hearing or discussing information, find a study partner who learns the same way or read aloud to yourself. Think about how to put the information in your own words. Imagine that you are giving a lecture on the topic and record yourself so you can listen to it later.

For any learning style, flashcards can be helpful. Organize the information so you can take advantage of spare moments to review. Underline key words or phrases. Use different colors for different categories. Mnemonic devices (such as creating a short list in which every item starts with the same letter) can also help with retention. Find what works best for you and use it to store the information in your mind most effectively and easily.

Secret Key #3 – Practice the Right Way

Your success on test day depends not only on how many hours you put into preparing, but also on whether you prepared the right way. It's good to check along the way to see if your studying is paying off. One of the most effective ways to do this is by taking practice tests to evaluate your progress. Practice tests are useful because they show exactly where you need to improve. Every time you take a practice test, pay special attention to these three groups of questions:

- The questions you got wrong
- The questions you had to guess on, even if you guessed right
- The questions you found difficult or slow to work through

This will show you exactly what your weak areas are, and where you need to devote more study time. Ask yourself why each of these questions gave you trouble. Was it because you didn't understand the material? Was it because you didn't remember the vocabulary? Do you need more repetitions on this type of question to build speed and confidence? Dig into those questions and figure out how you can strengthen your weak areas as you go back to review the material.

Additionally, many practice tests have a section explaining the answer choices. It can be tempting to read the explanation and think that you now have a good understanding of the concept. However, an explanation likely only covers part of the question's broader context. Even if the explanation makes perfect sense, **go back and investigate** every concept related to the question until you're positive you have a thorough understanding.

As you go along, keep in mind that the practice test is just that: practice. Memorizing these questions and answers will not be very helpful on the actual test because it is unlikely to have any of the same exact questions. If you only know the right answers to the sample questions, you won't be prepared for the real thing. **Study the concepts** until you understand them fully, and then you'll be able to answer any question that shows up on the test.

It's important to wait on the practice tests until you're ready. If you take a test on your first day of study, you may be overwhelmed by the amount of material covered and how much you need to learn. Work up to it gradually.

On test day, you'll need to be prepared for answering questions, managing your time, and using the test-taking strategies you've learned. It's a lot to balance, like a mental marathon that will have a big impact on your future. Like training for a marathon, you'll need to start slowly and work your way up. When test day arrives, you'll be ready.

Start with the strategies you've read in the first two Secret Keys—plan your course and study in the way that works best for you. If you have time, consider using multiple study resources to get different approaches to the same concepts. It can be helpful to see difficult concepts from more than one angle. Then find a good source for practice tests. Many times, the test website will suggest potential study resources or provide sample tests.

Practice Test Strategy

If you're able to find at least three practice tests, we recommend this strategy:

Untimed and Open-Book Practice

Take the first test with no time constraints and with your notes and study guide handy. Take your time and focus on applying the strategies you've learned.

Timed and Open-Book Practice

Take the second practice test open-book as well, but set a timer and practice pacing yourself to finish in time.

Timed and Closed-Book Practice

Take any other practice tests as if it were test day. Set a timer and put away your study materials. Sit at a table or desk in a quiet room, imagine yourself at the testing center, and answer questions as quickly and accurately as possible.

Keep repeating timed and closed-book tests on a regular basis until you run out of practice tests or it's time for the actual test. Your mind will be ready for the schedule and stress of test day, and you'll be able to focus on recalling the material you've learned.

Secret Key #4 – Pace Yourself

Once you're fully prepared for the material on the test, your biggest challenge on test day will be managing your time. Just knowing that the clock is ticking can make you panic even if you have plenty of time left. Work on pacing yourself so you can build confidence against the time constraints of the exam. Pacing is a difficult skill to master, especially in a high-pressure environment, so **practice is vital**.

Set time expectations for your pace based on how much time is available. For example, if a section has 60 questions and the time limit is 30 minutes, you know you have to average 30 seconds or less per question in order to answer them all. Although 30 seconds is the hard limit, set 25 seconds per question as your goal, so you reserve extra time to spend on harder questions. When you budget extra time for the harder questions, you no longer have any reason to stress when those questions take longer to answer.

Don't let this time expectation distract you from working through the test at a calm, steady pace, but keep it in mind so you don't spend too much time on any one question. Recognize that taking extra time on one question you don't understand may keep you from answering two that you do understand later in the test. If your time limit for a question is up and you're still not sure of the answer, mark it and move on, and come back to it later if the time and the test format allow. If the testing format doesn't allow you to return to earlier questions, just make an educated guess; then put it out of your mind and move on.

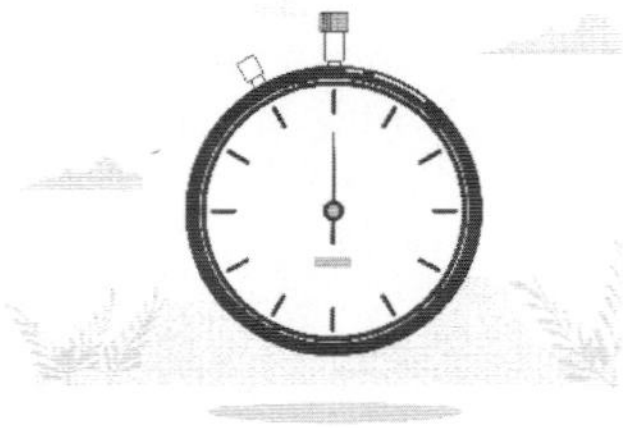

On the easier questions, be careful not to rush. It may seem wise to hurry through them so you have more time for the challenging ones, but it's not worth missing one if you know the concept and just didn't take the time to read the question fully. Work efficiently but make sure you understand the question and have looked at all of the answer choices, since more than one may seem right at first.

Even if you're paying attention to the time, you may find yourself a little behind at some point. You should speed up to get back on track, but do so wisely. Don't panic; just take a few seconds less on each question until you're caught up. Don't guess without thinking, but do look through the answer choices and eliminate any you know are wrong. If you can get down to two choices, it is often worthwhile to guess from those. Once you've chosen an answer, move on and don't dwell on any that you skipped or had to hurry through. If a question was taking too long, chances are it was one of the harder ones, so you weren't as likely to get it right anyway.

On the other hand, if you find yourself getting ahead of schedule, it may be beneficial to slow down a little. The more quickly you work, the more likely you are to make a careless mistake that will affect your score. You've budgeted time for each question, so don't be afraid to spend that time. Practice an efficient but careful pace to get the most out of the time you have.

Secret Key #5 – Have a Plan for Guessing

When you're taking the test, you may find yourself stuck on a question. Some of the answer choices seem better than others, but you don't see the one answer choice that is obviously correct. What do you do?

The scenario described above is very common, yet most test takers have not effectively prepared for it. Developing and practicing a plan for guessing may be one of the single most effective uses of your time as you get ready for the exam.

In developing your plan for guessing, there are three questions to address:

- When should you start the guessing process?
- How should you narrow down the choices?
- Which answer should you choose?

When to Start the Guessing Process

Unless your plan for guessing is to select C every time (which, despite its merits, is not what we recommend), you need to leave yourself enough time to apply your answer elimination strategies. Since you have a limited amount of time for each question, that means that if you're going to give yourself the best shot at guessing correctly, you have to decide quickly whether or not you will guess.

Of course, the best-case scenario is that you don't have to guess at all, so first, see if you can answer the question based on your knowledge of the subject and basic reasoning skills. Focus on the key words in the question and try to jog your memory of related topics. Give yourself a chance to bring the knowledge to mind, but once you realize that you don't have (or you can't access) the knowledge you need to answer the question, it's time to start the guessing process.

It's almost always better to start the guessing process too early than too late. It only takes a few seconds to remember something and answer the question from knowledge. Carefully eliminating wrong answer choices takes longer. Plus, going through the process of eliminating answer choices can actually help jog your memory.

Summary: Start the guessing process as soon as you decide that you can't answer the question based on your knowledge.

How to Narrow Down the Choices

The next chapter in this book (**Test-Taking Strategies**) includes a wide range of strategies for how to approach questions and how to look for answer choices to eliminate. You will definitely want to read those carefully, practice them, and figure out which ones work best for you. Here though, we're going to address a mindset rather than a particular strategy.

Your odds of guessing an answer correctly depend on how many options you are choosing from.

Number of options left	5	4	3	2	1
Odds of guessing correctly	20%	25%	33%	50%	100%

You can see from this chart just how valuable it is to be able to eliminate incorrect answers and make an educated guess, but there are two things that many test takers do that cause them to miss out on the benefits of guessing:

- Accidentally eliminating the correct answer
- Selecting an answer based on an impression

We'll look at the first one here, and the second one in the next section.

To avoid accidentally eliminating the correct answer, we recommend a thought exercise called **the $5 challenge**. In this challenge, you only eliminate an answer choice from contention if you are willing to bet $5 on it being wrong. Why $5? Five dollars is a small but not insignificant amount of money. It's an amount you could afford to lose but wouldn't want to throw away. And while losing $5 once might not hurt too much, doing it twenty times will set you back $100. In the same way, each small decision you make—eliminating a choice here, guessing on a question there—won't by itself impact your score very much, but when you put them all together, they can make a big difference. By holding each answer choice elimination decision to a higher standard, you can reduce the risk of accidentally eliminating the correct answer.

The $5 challenge can also be applied in a positive sense: If you are willing to bet $5 that an answer choice *is* correct, go ahead and mark it as correct.

Summary: Only eliminate an answer choice if you are willing to bet $5 that it is wrong.

Which Answer to Choose

You're taking the test. You've run into a hard question and decided you'll have to guess. You've eliminated all the answer choices you're willing to bet $5 on. Now you have to pick an answer. Why do we even need to talk about this? Why can't you just pick whichever one you feel like when the time comes?

The answer to these questions is that if you don't come into the test with a plan, you'll rely on your impression to select an answer choice, and if you do that, you risk falling into a trap. The test writers know that everyone who takes their test will be guessing on some of the questions, so they intentionally write wrong answer choices to seem plausible. You still have to pick an answer though, and if the wrong answer choices are designed to look right, how can you ever be sure that you're not falling for their trap? The best solution we've found to this dilemma is to take the decision out of your hands entirely. Here is the process we recommend:

Once you've eliminated any choices that you are confident (willing to bet $5) are wrong, select the first remaining choice as your answer.

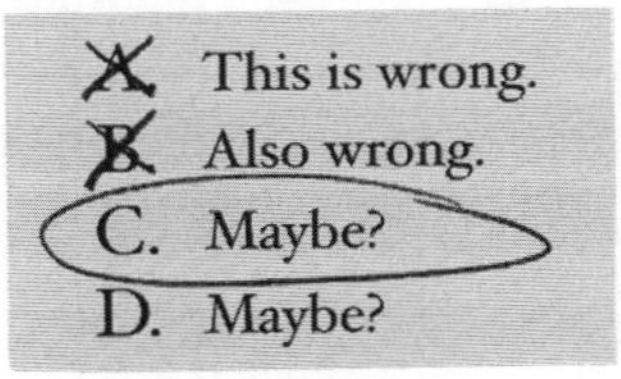

Whether you choose to select the first remaining choice, the second, or the last, the important thing is that you use some preselected standard. Using this approach guarantees that you will not be enticed into selecting an answer choice that looks right, because you are not basing your decision on how the answer choices look.

This is not meant to make you question your knowledge. Instead, it is to help you recognize the difference between your knowledge and your impressions. There's a huge difference between thinking an answer is right because of what you know, and thinking an answer is right because it looks or sounds like it should be right.

Summary: To ensure that your selection is appropriately random, make a predetermined selection from among all answer choices you have not eliminated.

Test-Taking Strategies

This section contains a list of test-taking strategies that you may find helpful as you work through the test. By taking what you know and applying logical thought, you can maximize your chances of answering any question correctly!

It is very important to realize that every question is different and every person is different: no single strategy will work on every question, and no single strategy will work for every person. That's why we've included all of them here, so you can try them out and determine which ones work best for different types of questions and which ones work best for you.

Question Strategies

✓ Read Carefully

Read the question and the answer choices carefully. Don't miss the question because you misread the terms. You have plenty of time to read each question thoroughly and make sure you understand what is being asked. Yet a happy medium must be attained, so don't waste too much time. You must read carefully and efficiently.

✓ Contextual Clues

Look for contextual clues. If the question includes a word you are not familiar with, look at the immediate context for some indication of what the word might mean. Contextual clues can often give you all the information you need to decipher the meaning of an unfamiliar word. Even if you can't determine the meaning, you may be able to narrow down the possibilities enough to make a solid guess at the answer to the question.

✓ Prefixes

If you're having trouble with a word in the question or answer choices, try dissecting it. Take advantage of every clue that the word might include. Prefixes can be a huge help. Usually, they allow you to determine a basic meaning. *Pre-* means before, *post-* means after, *pro-* is positive, *de-* is negative. From prefixes, you can get an idea of the general meaning of the word and try to put it into context.

✓ Hedge Words

Watch out for critical hedge words, such as *likely, may, can, often, almost, mostly, usually, generally, rarely*, and *sometimes*. Question writers insert these hedge phrases to cover every possibility. Often an answer choice will be wrong simply because it leaves no room for exception. Be on guard for answer choices that have definitive words such as *exactly* and *always*.

✓ Switchback Words

Stay alert for *switchbacks*. These are the words and phrases frequently used to alert you to shifts in thought. The most common switchback words are *but, although*, and *however*. Others include *nevertheless, on the other hand, even though, while, in spite of, despite*, and *regardless of*. Switchback words are important to catch because they can change the direction of the question or an answer choice.

⊘ FACE VALUE

When in doubt, use common sense. Accept the situation in the problem at face value. Don't read too much into it. These problems will not require you to make wild assumptions. If you have to go beyond creativity and warp time or space in order to have an answer choice fit the question, then you should move on and consider the other answer choices. These are normal problems rooted in reality. The applicable relationship or explanation may not be readily apparent, but it is there for you to figure out. Use your common sense to interpret anything that isn't clear.

Answer Choice Strategies

⊘ ANSWER SELECTION

The most thorough way to pick an answer choice is to identify and eliminate wrong answers until only one is left, then confirm it is the correct answer. Sometimes an answer choice may immediately seem right, but be careful. The test writers will usually put more than one reasonable answer choice on each question, so take a second to read all of them and make sure that the other choices are not equally obvious. As long as you have time left, it is better to read every answer choice than to pick the first one that looks right without checking the others.

⊘ ANSWER CHOICE FAMILIES

An answer choice family consists of two (in rare cases, three) answer choices that are very similar in construction and cannot all be true at the same time. If you see two answer choices that are direct opposites or parallels, one of them is usually the correct answer. For instance, if one answer choice says that quantity *x* increases and another either says that quantity *x* decreases (opposite) or says that quantity *y* increases (parallel), then those answer choices would fall into the same family. An answer choice that doesn't match the construction of the answer choice family is more likely to be incorrect. Most questions will not have answer choice families, but when they do appear, you should be prepared to recognize them.

⊘ ELIMINATE ANSWERS

Eliminate answer choices as soon as you realize they are wrong, but make sure you consider all possibilities. If you are eliminating answer choices and realize that the last one you are left with is also wrong, don't panic. Start over and consider each choice again. There may be something you missed the first time that you will realize on the second pass.

⊘ AVOID FACT TRAPS

Don't be distracted by an answer choice that is factually true but doesn't answer the question. You are looking for the choice that answers the question. Stay focused on what the question is asking for so you don't accidentally pick an answer that is true but incorrect. Always go back to the question and make sure the answer choice you've selected actually answers the question and is not merely a true statement.

⊘ EXTREME STATEMENTS

In general, you should avoid answers that put forth extreme actions as standard practice or proclaim controversial ideas as established fact. An answer choice that states the "process should be used in certain situations, if…" is much more likely to be correct than one that states the "process should be discontinued completely." The first is a calm rational statement and doesn't even make a definitive, uncompromising stance, using a hedge word *if* to provide wiggle room, whereas the second choice is far more extreme.

⊘ BENCHMARK

As you read through the answer choices and you come across one that seems to answer the question well, mentally select that answer choice. This is not your final answer, but it's the one that will help you evaluate the other answer choices. The one that you selected is your benchmark or standard for judging each of the other answer choices. Every other answer choice must be compared to your benchmark. That choice is correct until proven otherwise by another answer choice beating it. If you find a better answer, then that one becomes your new benchmark. Once you've decided that no other choice answers the question as well as your benchmark, you have your final answer.

⊘ PREDICT THE ANSWER

Before you even start looking at the answer choices, it is often best to try to predict the answer. When you come up with the answer on your own, it is easier to avoid distractions and traps because you will know exactly what to look for. The right answer choice is unlikely to be word-for-word what you came up with, but it should be a close match. Even if you are confident that you have the right answer, you should still take the time to read each option before moving on.

General Strategies

⊘ TOUGH QUESTIONS

If you are stumped on a problem or it appears too hard or too difficult, don't waste time. Move on! Remember though, if you can quickly check for obviously incorrect answer choices, your chances of guessing correctly are greatly improved. Before you completely give up, at least try to knock out a couple of possible answers. Eliminate what you can and then guess at the remaining answer choices before moving on.

⊘ CHECK YOUR WORK

Since you will probably not know every term listed and the answer to every question, it is important that you get credit for the ones that you do know. Don't miss any questions through careless mistakes. If at all possible, try to take a second to look back over your answer selection and make sure you've selected the correct answer choice and haven't made a costly careless mistake (such as marking an answer choice that you didn't mean to mark). This quick double check should more than pay for itself in caught mistakes for the time it costs.

⊘ PACE YOURSELF

It's easy to be overwhelmed when you're looking at a page full of questions; your mind is confused and full of random thoughts, and the clock is ticking down faster than you would like. Calm down and maintain the pace that you have set for yourself. Especially as you get down to the last few minutes of the test, don't let the small numbers on the clock make you panic. As long as you are on track by monitoring your pace, you are guaranteed to have time for each question.

⊘ DON'T RUSH

It is very easy to make errors when you are in a hurry. Maintaining a fast pace in answering questions is pointless if it makes you miss questions that you would have gotten right otherwise. Test writers like to include distracting information and wrong answers that seem right. Taking a little extra time to avoid careless mistakes can make all the difference in your test score. Find a pace that allows you to be confident in the answers that you select.

⊘ Keep Moving

Panicking will not help you pass the test, so do your best to stay calm and keep moving. Taking deep breaths and going through the answer elimination steps you practiced can help to break through a stress barrier and keep your pace.

Final Notes

The combination of a solid foundation of content knowledge and the confidence that comes from practicing your plan for applying that knowledge is the key to maximizing your performance on test day. As your foundation of content knowledge is built up and strengthened, you'll find that the strategies included in this chapter become more and more effective in helping you quickly sift through the distractions and traps of the test to isolate the correct answer.

Now that you're preparing to move forward into the test content chapters of this book, be sure to keep your goal in mind. As you read, think about how you will be able to apply this information on the test. If you've already seen sample questions for the test and you have an idea of the question format and style, try to come up with questions of your own that you can answer based on what you're reading. This will give you valuable practice applying your knowledge in the same ways you can expect to on test day.

Good luck and good studying!

Acids, Bases, and Salts

Acids and Bases

Several differences exist between acids and bases. Acidic solutions tend to taste sour, whereas basic solutions tend to taste bitter. Dilute bases tend to feel slippery, whereas dilute acids feel like water. Active metals such as magnesium and zinc react with acids to produce hydrogen gas, but active metals usually do not react with bases. Acids and bases form electrolytes in aqueous solutions and conduct electricity. Acids turn blue litmus red, but bases turn red litmus blue. Acidic solutions have a pH of less than 7, whereas basic solutions have a pH of greater than 7.

Acids or bases are categorized as strong or weak based on how completely they ionize in an aqueous solution. Strong acids and strong bases ionize essentially completely in an aqueous solution. Weak acids and weak bases ionize incompletely in an aqueous solution. Examples of strong acids include hydrochloric acid (HCl), sulfuric acid (H_2SO_4), and nitric acid (NO_3). Examples of weak acids are acetic acid ($HC_2H_3O_2$), hydrofluoric acid (HF), and carbonic acid (H_2CO_3). Examples of strong bases include sodium hydroxide (NaOH), potassium hydroxide (KOH), and calcium hydroxide ($Ca(OH)_2$). Ammonia (NH_3) is the most common weak base.

Arrhenius Acid and Base

Arrhenius acids are substances that produce hydrogen ions (H^+) when dissolved in water to form aqueous solutions. Arrhenius bases are substances that produce hydroxide ions (OH^-) when dissolved in water to form aqueous solutions. The Arrhenius concept is limited to acids and bases in aqueous solutions and cannot be applied to other solids, liquids, and gases. Examples of Arrhenius acids include hydrochloric acid (HCl) and sulfuric acid (H_2SO_4). Examples of Arrhenius bases include sodium hydroxide (NaOH) and magnesium hydroxide ($Mg(OH)_2$).

Brønsted–Lowry Acid and Base

The Brønsted–Lowry concept is based on the donation or the acceptance of a proton. According to the Brønsted–Lowry concept, an acid is a substance that donates one or more protons to another substance and a base is a substance that accepts a proton from another substance. The Brønsted–Lowry concept can be applied to substances other than aqueous solutions. This concept is much broader than the Arrhenius concept, which can only be applied to aqueous solutions. The Brønsted–Lowry concept states that a substance cannot act like an acid (donate its proton) unless another substance is available to act as a base (accept the donated proton). In this concept, water may act as either an acid or a base. Hydrochloric acid (HCl) is an example of a Brønsted–Lowry acid. Ammonia (NH_3) is an example of a Brønsted–Lowry base.

Lewis Acid and Base

A Lewis acid is any substance that can accept a pair of nonbonding electrons. A Lewis base is any substance that can donate a pair of nonbonding electrons. According to the Lewis theory, all cations such as Mg^{2+} and Cu^{2+} are Lewis acids. Trigonal planar molecules, which are exceptions to the octet rule such as BF_3, are Lewis acids. Molecules such as CO_2 that have multiple bonds between two atoms that differ in electronegativities are Lewis acids, also. According to the Lewis theory, all anions such as OH^- are Lewis bases. Other examples of Lewis bases include trigonal pyramidal molecules such as ammonia, NH_3, and nonmetal oxides such as carbon dioxide, CO_2. Some compounds such as water, H_2O, can be either Lewis acids or bases.

Neutralization Reaction

Neutralization is a reaction of an acid and a base that yields a salt and water. The salt is formed from the cation of the base and the anion of the acid. The water is formed from the cation of the acid and the anion of the base: acid + base → salt + water

An example is the neutralization reaction of hydrochloric acid and sodium hydroxide to form sodium chloride and water:

$$HCl\ (aq) + NaOH\ (aq) \rightarrow NaCl\ (s) + H_2O\ (l).$$

Equivalence Point

The *equivalence point* is by definition the point in a titration at which the analyte is neutralized. When the acid–base indicator starts to change color, the equivalence point has been reached. At this point, equivalent amounts of acids and bases have reacted. Also, at this point, $[H^+] = [OH^-]$. On an acid–base titration curve, the slope of the curve increases dramatically at the equivalence point. For strong acids and bases, the equivalence point occurs at a pH of 7. The figures below show the equivalence points for a strong acid titrated with a strong base (a) and a strong base titrated with a strong acid (b).

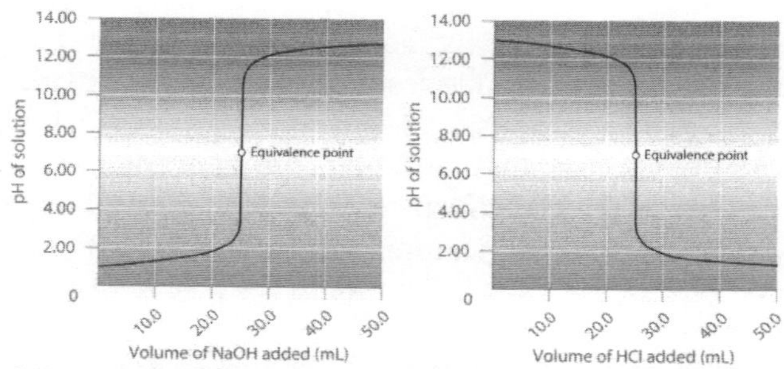

(a) Strong acid titrated with strong base (b) Strong base titrated with strong acid

pH Scale

The pH scale categorizes the acidity or alkalinity (basicity) of a solution. The pH value may be calculated by the formula $pH = -\log[H^+]$, where $[H^+]$ is the concentration of hydrogen ions. The pH scales ranges from 0 to 14 with pH values near zero indicating the strongest acids and pH values near 14 indicating the strongest bases. With the pH scale, any solution with a $pH < 7$ is considered an acid and any solution with a $pH > 7$ is considered a base. Solutions with a pH of 7 are considered to be neutral.

Relationship Between pH and pOH

The pH of a solution may be calculated using the formula $pH = -\log[H^+]$, where $[H^+]$ is the concentration of hydrogen ions. The pOH of a solution may be calculated using the formula $pOH = -\log[OH^-]$, where $[OH^-]$ is the concentration of hydroxide ions. The sum of the pH of a solution and the pOH of a solution is always 14. The pH of this HCl solution may be calculated using the formula $pH = -\log[0.0010\ M] = 3$. The sum of the pH and pOH is always 14. Therefore, the pOH may be calculated by the formula $14 - 3 = 11$.

How to Calculate $[H^+]$ and $[OH^-]$ When Given the pH or pOH

Because $pH = -\log[H^+]$, the $[H^+]$ may be calculated by $[H^+] = \text{antilog}(-pH)$. Because $pOH = -\log[OH^-]$, the $[OH^-]$ may be calculated by $[OH^-] = \text{antilog}(-pOH)$. Also, because the $pH + pOH = 14$, the pOH may be calculated by the formula 14 – pH = pOH. For example, given a solution with a pOH pf 8.0, the $[OH^-]$ = antilog (–8.0) = 1.0×10^{-8}. The pH = 14 – 8.0 = 6.0. The $[H^+]$ = antilog (–6.0) = 1×10^{-6}.

The Meaning of K_w

Pure water dissociates to a very small extent and reaches this equilibrium: $H_2O(l) + H_2O(l) \leftrightarrow H_3O^+(aq) + OH^-(aq)$. The equilibrium constant for this equilibrium is called the ion product constant of water, or K_w. The constant K_w can be represented by $K_w = [H_3O^+][OH^-]$. The reactant H_2O is not represented in the equilibrium expression because it is essentially a pure liquid. The ion product constant of water K_w varies with temperature. As temperature increases, K_w increases and pH decreases. Therefore, this constant must be given at a specific temperature. At 25 °C, $[H_3O^+] = [OH^-] = 1 \times 10^{-7}$ M, which corresponds to pure water being neutral with a pH of 7.

Acid–Base Indicators

Acid–base indicators are one method to determine the range of the pH of a solution. Acid– base indicators change with the pH of the solution and are less precise than using a pH meter. However, acid–base indicators are used to indicate the completion of a titration to determine the concentration of an acidic or basic solution. Examples of acid–base indicators include methyl violet, litmus, and phenolphthalein. Methyl violet turns from yellow to blue with a pH range of 0.0–1.6. Litmus turns from red to blue with a pH range of 4.5–8.3. Phenolphthalein turns from colorless to reddish purple with a pH range of 8.3–10.0.

Determining the Endpoint in a Titration

During a titration, when the acid–base indicator has fully changed color, the endpoint has been reached. If the proper acid–base indicator with the correct pH range has been used, this should also correspond to the equivalence point. For example, if trying to determine the pH of an unknown base using phenolphthalein, the solution should change from colorless to pink at the equivalence point. If trying to determine the pH of an unknown acid using methyl violet, the solution should change from yellow to blue at the equivalence point. However, the endpoint and the equivalence point are not necessarily equal. Ideally, the equivalence point is the endpoint. If the solution is overtitrated, the endpoint will be past the equivalence point.

Calculating the Unknown Concentration of a Base from a Titration

The unknown concentration of an acid or base may be determined by a titration. To determine the unknown concentration of a base, titrate a known volume of the base with an acid of known molarity. Use an acid–base indicator such as phenolphthalein to indicate when the titration has reached the equivalence point. If the solution is not overtitrated, the equivalence point will also be the endpoint. Then, calculate the concentration of the base using the formula $V_bN_b = V_aN_a$, where V_b represents the volume of the base, N_b represents the normality of the base, V_a represents the volume of the acid used in the titration, and N_a represents the normality of the acid used in the titration.

During a Titration, 20.0 mL of 0.0100 M NaOH is Required to Neutralize a 50.0 mL Sample of HCl Solution. Explain How to Find the Molarity of the HCl.

To find the concentration of the unknown acid, use the formula $V_bN_b = V_aN_a$, where V_b represents the volume of the base, N_b represents the normality of the base, V_a represents the volume of the acid, and N_a represents the normality of the acid used in the titration. Solving the equation for the variable N_a yields $N_a = \frac{V_bN_b}{V_a}$. Because the molarity of the NaOH is 0.0100 M, the normality of the

NAOH is 0.0100 N. Substituting in the appropriate values into the formula yields $N_a = \frac{(20.0\text{ mL})(0.0100\text{ N})}{50.0\text{ mL}} = 0.00400$ N. Because HCl is monoprotic, the molarity of HCl is 0.00400 M.

Monoprotic and Polyprotic Acids

Monoprotic acids are acids that have only one proton available to donate. Polyprotic acids have two or more protons available to donate. Typically, polyprotic acids donate their available protons in stages of one at a time. Specifically, diprotic acids can donate two protons, and triprotic acids can donate three protons. Common monoprotic acids include hydrochloric acid (HCl) and nitric acid (HNO_3). Common diprotic acids include sulfuric acid (H_2SO_4) and sulfurous acid (H_2SO_3). Phosphoric acid (H_3PO_4) is a common triprotic acid.

K_A of an Acid and the K_B of a Base

Given this general form for equilibrium of an acid in aqueous solution, HA (aq) + H_2O (l) ↔ H_3O^+ (aq) + A^- (aq), the equilibrium constant expression is called the acid dissociation constant, K_a:

$$K_a = \frac{[H_3O^+][A^-]}{[HA]}.$$

Strong acids have high K_a values because strong acids ionize essentially completely in aqueous solution. Weak acids have low K_a values because weak acids do not ionize completely in aqueous solution.

Given this general form for equilibrium of a base in aqueous solution, B (aq) + H_2O (l) ↔ BH^+ (aq) + OH^- (aq), the equilibrium constant expression is called the base dissociation constant, K_b:

$$K_b = \frac{[BH^+][OH^-]}{[B]}.$$

Strong bases have high K_b values because strong bases ionize essentially completely in aqueous solution. Weak bases have low K_b values because weak bases do not ionize completely in aqueous solution.

Hydrolysis

Hydrolysis is a chemical reaction between water and another reactant in which both compounds split apart. The water molecules split into hydrogen ions (H^+) and hydroxide ions (OH^-). The other compound splits into a cation and anion, too. Another way to state this is that hydrolysis is a decomposition reaction of a compound that is combined with water. The general form of a hydrolysis reaction is given by X– (aq) + H_2O (l) ↔ HX (aq) + OH^- (aq). A salt hydrolysis reaction is the reverse process of a neutralization reaction. A neutralization reaction is given by the general form: acid + base → salt + water. In general, a salt hydrolysis reaction may be thought of as salt + water → acid + base.

Buffer Solution

A buffer solution is an aqueous solution that helps keep the pH highly constant. The addition of an acid or base to a buffer solution will not greatly affect the pH of that solution. A buffer consists of a weak acid and its conjugate base or a weak base and its conjugate acid. This combination of substances can remain in solution with each other without neutralizing each other. When acids or hydrogen ions (H^+) are added to a buffer solution, they are neutralized by the base in the buffer solution. When bases or hydroxide ions (OH^-) are added to a buffer solution, they are neutralized by the acid in the buffer solution.

Atomic Concepts

Subatomic Particles

The three major subatomic particles are the proton, neutron, and electron. The proton, which is located in the nucleus, has a relative charge of +1. The neutron, which is located in the nucleus, has a relative charge of 0. The electron, which is located outside the nucleus, has a relative charge of −1. The proton and neutron, which are essentially the same mass, are much more massive than the electron and make up the mass of the atom. The electron's mass is insignificant compared to the mass of the proton and neutron.

Orbits and Orbitals

An orbit is a definite path, but an orbital is a region in space. The Bohr model described electrons as orbiting or following a definite path in space around the nucleus of an atom. But, according to the uncertainty principle, it is impossible to determine the location and the momentum of an electron simultaneously. Therefore, it is impossible to draw a definite path or orbit of an electron. An orbital as described by the quantum-mechanical model or the electron-cloud model is a region in space that is drawn in such a way as to indicate the probability of finding an electron at a specific location. The distance an orbital is located from the nucleus corresponds to the principal quantum number. The orbital shape corresponds to the subshell or azimuthal quantum number. The orbital orientation corresponds to the magnetic quantum number.

Quantum Numbers

The principal quantum number (n) describes an electron's shell or energy level and actually describes the size of the orbital. Electrons farther from the nucleus are at higher energy levels. The subshell or azimuthal quantum number (l) describes the electron's sublevel or subshell (s, *p*, *d*, or *f*) and specifies the shape of the orbital. Typical shapes include spherical, dumbbell, and clover leaf. The magnetic quantum number (m_l) describes the orientation of the orbital in space. The spin or magnetic moment quantum number (m_s) describes the direction of the spin of the electron in the orbital.

Cathode Ray Tube (CRT)

Electrons were discovered by Joseph John Thomson through scientific work with CRTs. Cathode rays had been studied for many years, but it was Thomson who showed that cathode rays were negatively charged particles. Although Thomson could not determine an electron's charge or mass, he was able to determine the ratio of the charge to the mass. Thomson discovered that this ratio was constant regardless of the gas in the CRT. He was able to show that the cathode rays were actually streams of negatively charged particles by deflecting them with a positively charged plate.

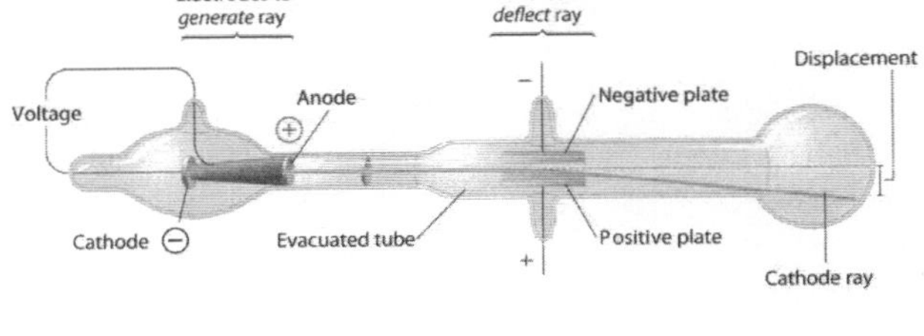

GOLD FOIL EXPERIMENT

After Thomson determined the ratio of the charge to the mass of an electron from studying cathode rays, he proposed the plum pudding model, in which he compared electrons to the raisins embedded in plum pudding. This model of the atom was disproved by the gold foil experiment. The gold foil experiment led to the discovery of the nucleus of an atom. Scientists at Rutherford's laboratory bombarded a thin gold foil with high-speed helium ions. Much to their surprise, some of the ions were reflected by the foil. The scientists concluded that the atom has a hard central core, which we now know to be the nucleus.

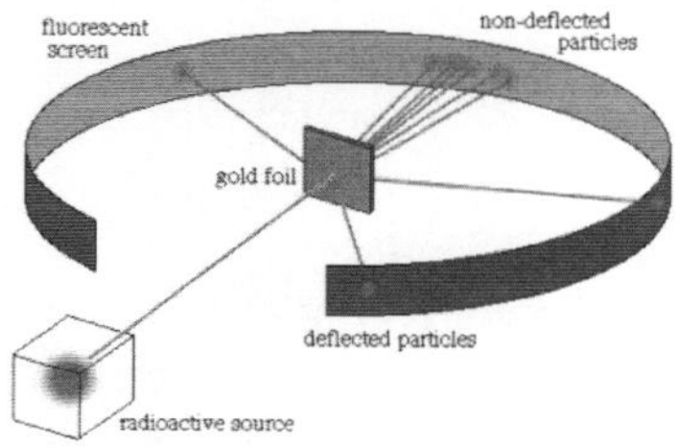

PROBLEMS THAT RUTHERFORD'S MODEL HAD WITH SPECTRAL LINES

Rutherford's model allowed for the electrons of an atom to be in an infinite number of orbits based on Newton's laws of motion. Rutherford believed that electrons could orbit the nucleus at any distance from the nucleus and that electrons could change velocity and direction at any moment. But, according to Rutherford's model, the electrons would lose energy and spiral into the nucleus. Unfortunately, if this was in fact true, then every atom would be unstable. Rutherford's model also does not correspond to the spectral lines emitted from gases at low pressure. The spectral lines are discrete bands of light at specific energy levels. These spectral lines indicate that electrons must be at specific distances from the nucleus. If electrons could be located at any distance from the nucleus, then these gases should emit continuous spectra instead of spectral lines.

ATOMIC NUMBER AND MASS NUMBER

The atomic number of an element is the number of protons in the nucleus of an atom of that element. This is the number that identifies the type of an atom. For example, all oxygen atoms have eight protons, and all carbon atoms have six protons. Each element is identified by its specific atomic number. The mass number is the number of protons and neutrons in the nucleus of an atom. Although the atomic number is the same for all atoms of a specific element, the mass number can vary due to the varying numbers of neutrons in various isotopes of the atom.

ISOTOPE

Isotopes are atoms of the same element that vary in their number of neutrons. Isotopes of the same element have the same number of protons and thus the same atomic number. But, because isotopes vary in the number of neutrons, they can be identified by their mass numbers. For example, two naturally occurring carbon isotopes are carbon-12 and carbon-13, which have mass numbers 12 and 13, respectively. The symbols ${}^{12}_{6}\mathrm{C}$ and ${}^{13}_{6}\mathrm{C}$ also represent the carbon isotopes. The general form of the symbol is ${}^{M}_{A}X$, where X represents the element symbol, M represents the mass number, and A represents the atomic number.

AVERAGE ATOMIC MASS

The *average atomic mass* is the weighted average of the masses of all the naturally occurring isotopes of an atom in comparison to the carbon-12 isotope. The unit for average atomic mass is the atomic mass unit (u). Atomic masses of isotopes are measured using a mass spectrometer by bombarding a gaseous sample of the isotope and measuring its relative deflections. Atomic masses can be calculated if the percent abundances and the atomic masses of the naturally occurring isotopes are known.

AUFBAU PRINCIPLE

The *Aufbau principle* is named from the German word for "building up," and it describes how electrons fill the energy levels or shells of an atom. In general, electrons will fill the $n = 1$ energy level before filling the $n = 2$ energy level, and electrons will fill the $n = 2$ energy level before filling the $n = 3$ energy level. The *s* subshell of an energy level will fill before the *p* subshell, which fills before the *d* and *f* subshells.

HUND'S RULE

Hund's rule describes how electrons fill the orbitals in a sublevel. Less energy is required for an electron to occupy an orbital alone than the energy needed for an electron to pair up with another electron in an orbital. Therefore, electrons will occupy each orbital in a subshell before electrons will begin to pair up in those orbitals. For example, in the 2*p* subshell, one electron will occupy each of the three orbitals before pairing begins. In the 3*d* subshell, one electron will occupy each of the five orbitals before pairing begins.

PAULI EXCLUSION PRINCIPLE

The *Pauli exclusion principle* describes the unique address or location of each electron in an atom. Each electron has a unique or exclusive set of four quantum numbers indicating the electron's energy level, subshell, orbital orientation, and magnetic moment. Every orbital can hold a maximum of two electrons, but even if two electrons occupy the same orbital resulting in identical energy levels, subshells, and orbital orientations, they must have opposite spins, which means that their magnetic moment quantum numbers will differ.

ELECTRON CONFIGURATION AND THE PERIODIC TABLE

Electron configurations show a direct correlation to the periodic table. The periodic table can be divided into blocks representing *s, p, d,* and *f* subshells. The energy level corresponds to the row or period of the periodic table. The subshells, *s, p, d,* or *f* are related to the block's group numbers. The *s* block corresponds to groups 1A and 2A. The *p* block corresponds to groups 3A–8A. The *d* block corresponds to the 10 groups of transition metals, and the *f* block corresponds to the two rows of inner transition metals (14 groups) located at the bottom of the table.

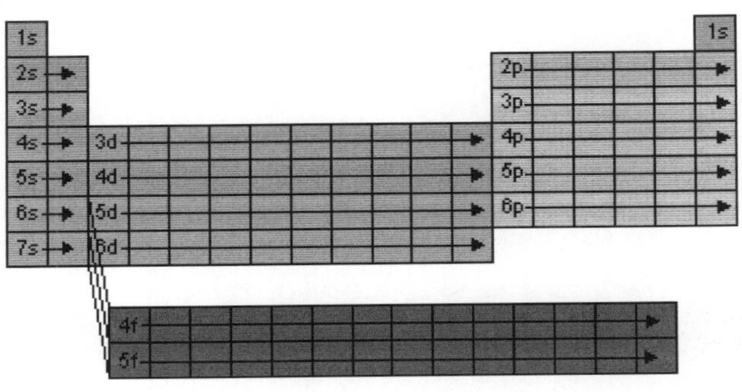

Relationship between electron configuration and chemical and physical properties (1)

ELECTRON CONFIGURATION AND CHEMICAL AND PHYSICAL PROPERTIES

The chemical and physical properties of atoms are related to the number of valence electrons the atom possesses. Atoms (except hydrogen and helium) seek to have eight electrons in their outer shell as stated in the octet rule. A full octet corresponds to full *s* and *p* orbitals. Noble gases all have full *s* and *p* orbitals and are inert. To fulfill the octet rule, elements in groups 1A (alkali metals) and 2A (alkaline earth metals) tend to lose one or two electrons, respectively, forming cations. Elements in group 6A (chalcogens) and group 7A (halogens) tend to gain one or two electrons, respectively, forming anions. Other elements such as carbon (group 4A) tend to form covalent bonds to satisfy the octet rule.

Chemical Bonding

Chemical and Physical Properties

Matter has both physical and chemical properties. Physical properties can be seen or observed without changing the identity or composition of matter. For example, the mass, volume, and density of a substance can be determined without permanently changing the sample. Other physical properties include color, boiling point, freezing point, solubility, odor, hardness, electrical conductivity, thermal conductivity, ductility, and malleability. Chemical properties cannot be measured without changing the identity or composition of matter. Chemical properties describe how a substance reacts or changes to form a new substance. Examples of chemical properties include flammability, corrosivity, oxidation states, enthalpy of formation, and reactivity with other chemicals.

Chemical and Physical Changes

Physical changes do not produce new substances. The atoms or molecules may be rearranged, but no new substances are formed. Phase changes or changes of state such as melting, freezing, and sublimation are physical changes. For example, physical changes include the melting of ice, the boiling of water, sugar dissolving into water, and the crushing of a piece of chalk into a fine powder. Chemical changes involve a chemical reaction and do produce new substances. When iron rusts, iron oxide is formed, indicating a chemical change. Other examples of chemical changes include baking a cake, burning wood, digesting a cracker, and mixing an acid and a base.

Intensive and Extensive Properties

Physical properties are categorized as either intensive or extensive. Intensive properties *do not* depend on the amount of matter or quantity of the sample. This means that intensive properties will not change if the sample size is increased or decreased. Intensive properties include color, hardness, melting point, boiling point, density, ductility, malleability, specific heat, temperature, concentration, and magnetization. Extensive properties *do* depend on the amount of matter or quantity of the sample. Therefore, extensive properties do change if the sample size is increased or decreased. If the sample size is increased, the property increases. If the sample size is decreased, the property decreases. Extensive properties include volume, mass, weight, energy, entropy, number of moles, and electrical charge.

Bonds

Chemical bonds are the attractive forces that bind atoms together into molecules. Atoms form chemical bonds in an attempt to satisfy the octet rule. These bond types include covalent bonds, ionic bonds, and metallic bonds. Covalent bonds are formed from the sharing of electron pairs between two atoms in a molecule. Ionic bonds are formed from the transferring of electrons between one atom and another, which results in the formations of cations and anions. Metallic bonding results from the sharing of delocalized electrons among all of the atoms in a molecule.

Polar covalent bonds result when electrons are shared unequally between atoms. Nonpolar covalent bonds result when electrons are shared equally between atoms. The unequal sharing of electrons is due to the differences in the electronegativities of the two atoms sharing the electrons. Partial charges develop due to this unequal sharing of electrons. The greater that the difference is in the electronegativities between the two atoms, the stronger the dipole is. For example, the covalent bonds formed between the carbon atom and the two oxygen atoms in carbon dioxide are polar covalent bonds because the electronegativities of carbon and oxygen differ slightly. If the electronegativities are equal, then the covalent bonds are nonpolar. For example, the covalent double bond between two oxygen atoms is nonpolar because the oxygen atoms have the same electronegativities.

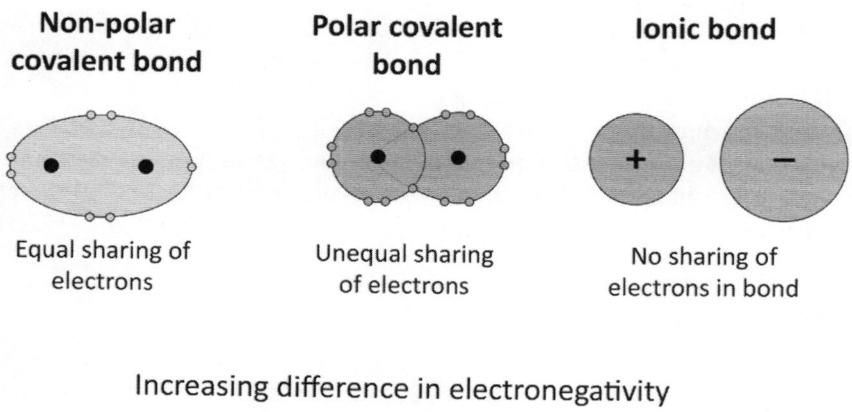

Covalent Bonds

Covalent bonding results from the sharing of electrons between atoms. Atoms seek to fill their valence shell and will share electrons with another atom in order to have a full octet (except hydrogen and helium, which only hold two electrons in their valence shells). Molecular compounds have covalent bonds. Organic compounds such as proteins, carbohydrates, lipids, and nucleic acids are molecular compounds formed by covalent bonds. Methane (CH_4) is a molecular compound in which one carbon atom is covalently bonded to four hydrogen atoms as shown below.

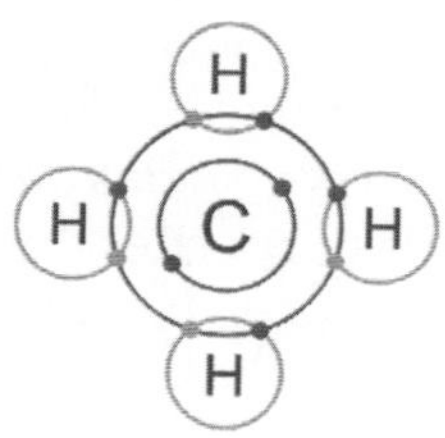

The bond length of a covalent bond is the distance between the nuclei of two covalently bonded atoms. The higher the bond order, the shorter the bond length. Single bonds are between one pair of electrons, and they are the weakest. Because single bonds (bond order 1) are the weakest, they are the longest of the three types of covalent bonds. Double bonds are between two pairs of electrons. Because double bonds (bond order 2) are stronger that single bonds, double bonds are shorter than single bonds. Triple bonds are between three pairs of electrons. Because triple bonds (bond order 3) are stronger than double bonds and single bonds, triple bonds have the shortest bond length.

The bond strength determines the amount of energy needed to break a covalent bond. Bond strength increases as bond length decreases. The bond length is the distance between the nuclei of two covalently bonded atoms. The higher the bond order, the shorter the bond length. Single bonds are between one pair of electrons, and they are the weakest. Double bonds are between two pairs of electrons. Double bonds (bond order 2) are stronger that single bonds. Triple bonds are between three pairs of electrons. Triple bonds (bond order 3) are stronger than double bonds and single bonds.

METALLIC BONDING

Metallic bonding is a type of bonding between metals. Metallic bonds are similar to covalent bonds in that they are a type of sharing of electrons between atoms. However, in covalent bonding, the electrons are shared with only one other atom. In metallic bonding, the electrons are shared with all the surrounding atoms. These electrons are referred to as delocalized electrons. Metallic bonding is responsible for many of the characteristics in metals including conductivity of heat and electricity, malleability, and ductility. An example of metallic bonding is the metallic bond between the copper atoms in a piece of copper wire.

IONIC BONDING

Ionic bonding results from the transfer of electrons between atoms. A cation or positive ion is formed when an atom loses one or more electrons. An anion or negative ion is formed when an atom gains one or more electrons. An ionic bond results from the electrostatic attraction between a cation and an anion. One example of a compound formed by ionic bonds is sodium chloride or NaCl. Sodium (Na) is an alkali metal and tends to form Na^+ ions. Chlorine is a halogen and tends to form Cl^- ions. The Na^+ ion and the Cl^- ion are attracted to each other. This electrostatic attraction between these oppositely charged ions is what results in the ionic bond between them.

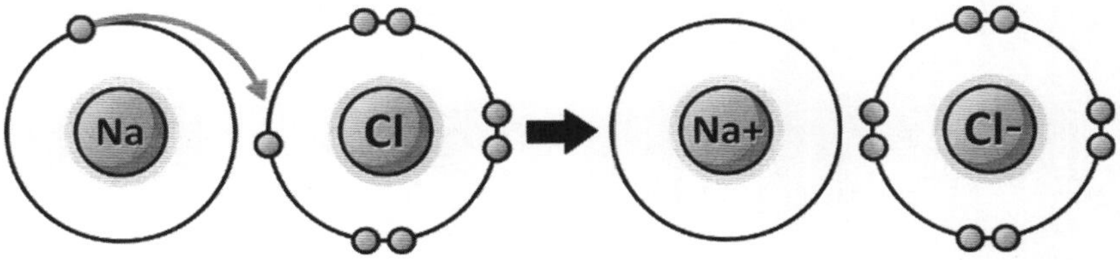

DRAWING A LEWIS STRUCTURE

In order to draw a Lewis structure for a molecule, determine the number of valence electrons for each atom in the molecule and the number of valence electrons each atom needs in order to have a full outer shell. All atoms except hydrogen and helium seek to have eight electrons in their outer shells. Hydrogen and helium only have room for two valence electrons. Next, determine the central atom. Usually, the central atom is the atom with the largest number of valence openings. Draw the skeletal structure with the central atom. Each single bond represents two electrons. Each double bond represents four electrons. Each triple bond represents six electrons. Start with single bonds and change to double or triple bonds as needed to satisfy the octet rule. But remember, atoms may only share what they have available. For example, elements in group IIIA have three valence electrons and need an additional five electrons to make eight, but they may only share the three that they have available. Add the remaining valence electrons to all the atoms. Check to make sure that each atom (except hydrogen, helium, and boron) satisfies the octet rule.

Example Lewis Structures

NH_3

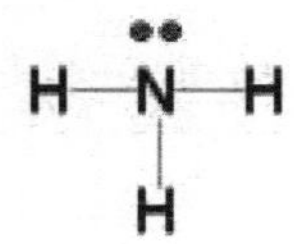

H_2O

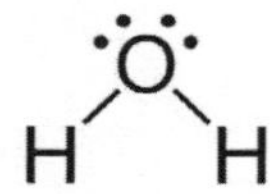

CCl_4

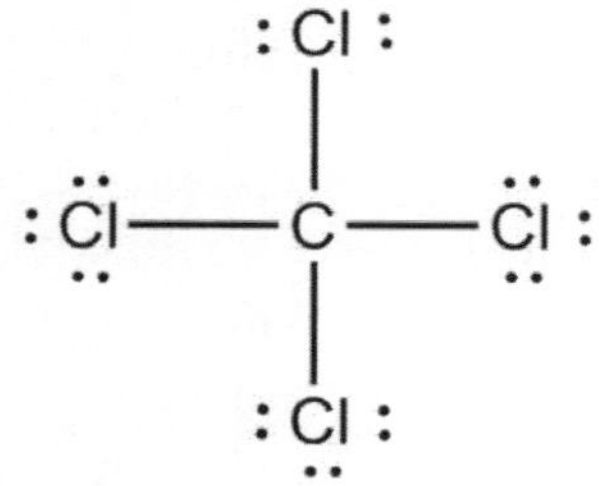

BF_3

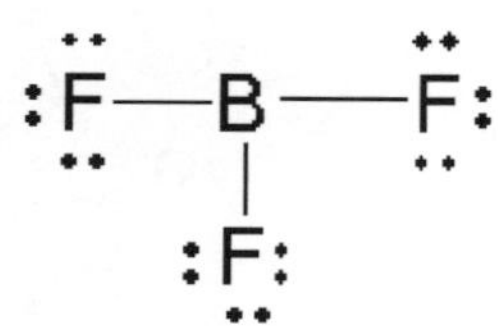

Resonance Structures

For some molecules, more than one Lewis structure may be drawn due to the delocalization of electrons. In order to determine which resonance structure is the most stable, calculate the formal charge of each structure. The structure with the lowest formal charge is the most stable. The actual molecule is a hybrid of all the possible Lewis structures. An example of resonance occurs in benzene, C_6H_6. The two possible Lewis structures for benzene are shown below. The only difference between the two Lewis structures is the placement of the single and double bonds between the carbon atoms.

Studies show that in reality, neither Lewis structure is correct. In fact, all the bonds between the carbon atoms are exactly the same. The structure of the resonance hybrid of benzene is often represented by the drawing shown below. The circle inside the ring of carbons represents the delocalized electrons that are shared among all the carbon atoms of the ring.

Possible Lewis Structures - Resonance Hybrid

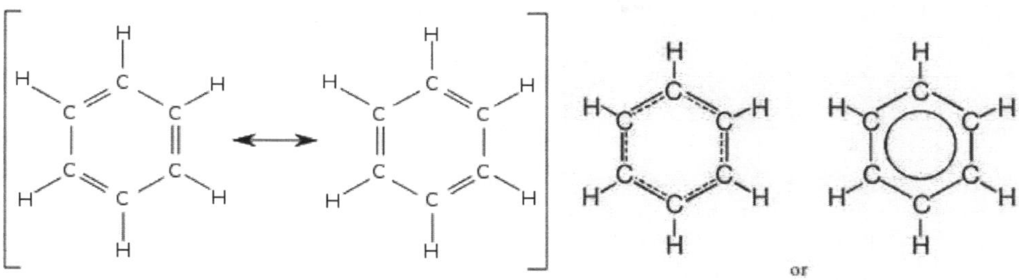

Molecular geometries

Linear — All diatomic molecules are linear molecules. Also, molecules with two bonding groups and two nonbonding pairs of electrons are linear. The bond angle measurement for linear molecules is 180°.

Trigonal planar — For a trigonal planar molecule, the central atom has three bonding pairs of electrons and zero nonbonding pairs. These molecules are an exception to the octet rule. The bond angle measurement for trigonal planar molecules is 120°.

Angular — For an angular molecule, the central atom has two bonding pairs of electrons and two nonbonding pairs. The bond angle measurement for angular molecules is less than 120°.

Tetrahedral — For a tetrahedral molecule, the central atom has four bonding pairs of electrons and zero nonbonding pairs. The bond angle measurement for tetrahedral molecules is 109.5°.

Trigonal pyramidal — For a trigonal pyramidal molecule, the central atom has three bonding pairs and one nonbonding pair. The bond angle measurement for trigonal pyramidal molecules is less than 109.5°.

Examples

Linear — Nitric oxide (NO) is another name for nitrogen monoxide. All diatomic molecules are linear.

Trigonal planar — Boron trifluoride (BF_3) has three bonding pairs and zero nonbonding pairs around the central atom. Therefore, boron trifluoride is trigonal planar.

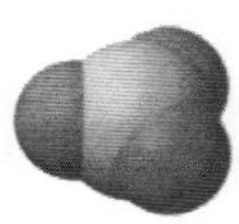

Angular or bent — Oxygen difluoride (OF_2) has two bonding pairs and zero nonbonding pairs around the central angle. Therefore, oxygen difluoride is angular or bent.

Tetrahedral — Methane (CH_4) has four bonding pairs and zero nonbonding pairs around the central angle. Therefore, methane is tetrahedral.

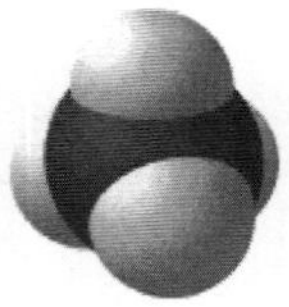

Ammonia — Ammonia (NH_3) has three bonding pairs and one bonding pair around the central atom. Therefore, ammonia is trigonal pyramidal.

Polar and Nonpolar Molecules

Covalently bonded molecules are either polar or nonpolar depending on the type and arrangement of their covalent bonds. Covalent bonds are polar if the electronegativities of the two atoms sharing the pair of electron differ. With differing electronegativities, the electrons are shared unequally with the pair of electrons displaced more toward the more electronegative atom. This results in a polar covalent bond. Covalent molecules always have polar covalent bonds. If the bonds are arranged symmetrically around a central atom, the polar bonds will "cancel" each other out resulting in a nonpolar molecule. If a molecule contains polar covalent bonds that are not arranged symmetrically in a way to "cancel" each other out, the molecule is polar. Molecules with only nonpolar covalent bonds are always nonpolar. Only molecules with polar covalent bonds can be polar.

Examples

CH_4 — Nonpolar: Methane or CH_4 has a tetrahedral geometry with four hydrogen atoms covalently bonded around the central carbon atom. These four bonds are polar covalent bonds, but because they are arranged symmetrically around the central carbon atom, the molecule is nonpolar.

CO_2 — Nonpolar: Carbon dioxide, or CO_2, is a linear molecule with two oxygen atoms covalently double bonded to a central carbon atom. These two double bonds are polar covalent bonds, but because they are arranged symmetrically around the carbon atom, the molecule is nonpolar.

H_2S — Polar: Dihydrogen sulfide, or H_2S, is an angular molecule with the two hydrogen atoms covalently bonded to a sulfur atom. This molecule has two bonding pairs and one nonbonding pair. Because of the nonbonding pair, the molecule is bent or angular. Because the polar bonds do not cancel each other out in this arrangement, the molecule is polar.

NH_3 — Polar: Ammonia, or NH_3, is a trigonal pyramidal molecule with the three hydrogen atoms bonded asymmetrically around the central nitrogen atom. The molecule has three bonding pairs and one nonbonding pair of electrons. Because the polar covalent bonds are arranged asymmetrically, the molecule is polar.

BF_3 – Nonpolar: Boron trifluoride is a trigonal planar molecule with three fluorine atoms bonded symmetrically around the central boron atom. Because the molecule is an exception to the octet rule and only has three bonding pairs and no nonbonding pairs around the central boron atom, these fluorine atoms are arranged symmetrically around the boron atom canceling out the effect of the polar covalent bonds and resulting in a nonpolar molecule.

Kinetics/Equilibrium

Laws of Thermodynamics

The zeroth law of thermodynamics describes the heat flow between three systems. If two systems are in equilibrium with a third system, then those two systems are in equilibrium with each other.

The first law of thermodynamics describes the internal energy of a system in relation to the heat and work added and or removed from that system. The first law of thermodynamics is represented by the equation $\Delta E = q + w$, where ΔE is the change in internal energy, q is the heat added to the system, and w is the work done on the system.

The second law of thermodynamics describes the entropy of a system in relation to absolute temperature. The second law of thermodynamics is represented by the equation $\Delta S = \frac{Q}{T}$, where ΔS is the change in entropy of the system, Q is the heat added or removed from the system, and T is the absolute temperature.

The Third law of thermodynamics describes the entropy of crystals at extremely low temperatures. The entropy of a pure crystal approaches zero as the temperature of the crystal approaches absolute zero.

Spontaneous/Reversible Processes

Some chemical processes are spontaneous. According to the second law of thermodynamics, systems or processes always tend to a state of greater entropy or lower potential energy. Some exothermic chemical systems are spontaneous because they can increase their stability by reaching a lower potential energy. If processes or reactions have products at a lower potential energy, these processes tend to be spontaneous. Spontaneous reactions have only one direction as given by the second law of thermodynamics. Spontaneous processes go in the direction of greater entropy and lower potential energy. To be reversible, a reaction or process has to be able to go back and forth the between two states. A spontaneous process is irreversible.

Entropy

Entropy (S) is the amount of disorder or randomness of a system. According to the second law of thermodynamics, systems tend toward a state of greater entropy. The second law of thermodynamics can also be stated as $\Delta S > 0$. Processes with positive changes in entropy tend to be spontaneous. For example, melting is a process with a positive ΔS. When a solid changes into a liquid state, the substance becomes more disordered; therefore, entropy increases. Entropy also will increase in a reaction in which the number of moles of gases increases due to the amount of disorder increasing. Entropy increases when a solute dissolves into a solvent due to the increase in the number of particles. Entropy increases when a system is heated due to the particles moving faster and the amount of disorder increasing.

ENTHALPY

All chemical processes involve either the release or the absorption of heat. Enthalpy is this heat energy. Enthalpy is a state function that is equivalent to the amount of heat a system exchanges with its surroundings. For exothermic processes, which release heat, the change in enthalpy (ΔH) is negative because the final enthalpy is less than the initial enthalpy. For endothermic processes, which absorb heat, the change in enthalpy (ΔH) is positive because the final enthalpy is greater than the initial enthalpy.

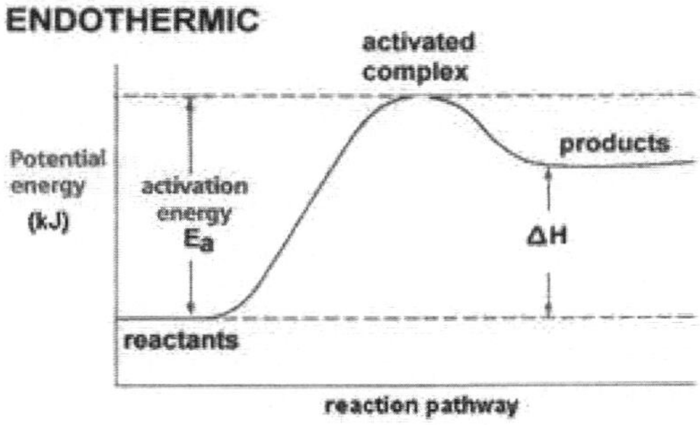

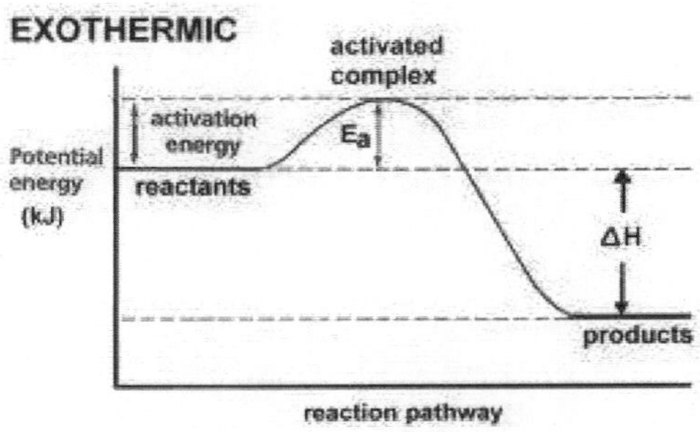

GIBBS ENERGY

Gibbs energy (G), also known as Gibbs free energy, is the energy of the system that is available to do work. Gibbs energy determines the spontaneity of chemical and physical processes. Some processes are spontaneous because $\Delta H < 0$ or because $\Delta S > 0$. If one of the conditions is favorable but the other condition is not favorable, Gibbs energy can be used to determine if a process is spontaneous. Gibbs energy is given by $G = H - TS$. For processes that occur at constant temperature, $\Delta G = \Delta H - T\Delta S$. If ΔG is equal to zero, then the reaction is at equilibrium and neither the forward nor the reverse reaction is spontaneous. If ΔG is less than zero, then the forward reaction is spontaneous. If ΔG is greater than zero, then the reverse reaction is spontaneous.

CHEMICAL KINETICS

Chemical kinetics is the study of the rates or speeds of chemical reactions and the various factors that affect these rates or speeds. The rate or speed of a reaction is the change in concentration of the reactant(s) or product(s) per unit of time. Another way to state this is that chemical kinetics is study of the rate of change of the concentrations of the reactant(s) and product(s) and the factors that affect that rate of change. The study of catalysts is part of chemical kinetics. Catalysts are substances that speed up the rate of reactions without being consumed. Examples of reactions that occur at different rates include the explosion of trinitrotoluene (TNT), which occurs at a very fast rate, compared to the burning of a log, which occurs at a much slower rate.

Give the rate law for this general reaction: aA + bB + cC ... → products.

The rate of a chemical reaction can be defined as the following:

$$\text{rate} = \frac{\text{change in concentration}}{\text{change in time}}.$$

This is usually represented by a rate law. The rate law for the general reaction aA + bB + cC... → products is given by rate = $k[A]^x[B]^y[C]^z$, where k is the rate constant; [A], [B], and [C] represent the concentrations of the reactants; and x, y, and z represent the reaction orders. The exponents x, y, and z must be experimentally determined. They do not necessarily equal the coefficients from the balanced chemical equation.

Activation Energy

Activation energy is the minimum amount of energy that must be possessed by reactant atoms or molecules in order to react. This is due to the fact that it takes a certain amount of energy to break bonds or form bonds between atoms. Reactants lacking the activation energy required will not be able to perform the necessary breaking or forming of bonds regardless of how often they collide. Catalysts lower the activation energy of a reaction and therefore increase the rate of reaction.

Reaction Mechanism

Often, when studying specific reactions, only the net reactions are given. Realistically, reactions take place in a series of steps or elementary reactions as shown in the reaction mechanism. Reaction mechanisms show how a reaction proceeds in a series of steps. Some steps are slow, and some are fast. Each step has its own reaction mechanism. The slowest step in the reaction mechanism coincides with the step with the greatest activation energy. This step is known as the rate-determining step.

Catalyst

A catalyst is a chemical that accelerates or speeds up a chemical reaction without being consumed or used up in the reaction. Although catalysts are not consumed or permanently changed during the process of the reaction, catalysts do participate in the elementary reaction of the reaction mechanisms. Catalysts cannot make an impossible reaction take place, but catalysts do greatly increase the rate of a reaction. Catalysts lower the activation energy. Because the activation energy is the minimum energy required for molecules to react, lowering the activation energy makes it possible for more of the reactant molecules to react.

Reaction Rate

Factors that affect reaction rate include concentration, surface area, and temperature. Increasing the concentration of the reactants increases the number of collisions between those reactants and therefore increases the reaction rate. Increasing the surface area of contact between the reactants also increases the number of collisions and therefore increases the reaction rate. Finally, increasing the temperature of the reactants increases the number of collisions but more significantly also increases the kinetic energy of the reactants, which in turn increases the fraction of molecules meeting activation energy requirement. With more molecules at the activation energy, more of the reactants are capable of completing the reaction.

Chemical Equilibrium

A chemical equilibrium occurs when a reaction is reversible and the rate of the forward reaction equals the rate of the reverse reaction. The forward and reverse reactions are continually occurring, but the individual concentration of the reaction and the products do not change. The concentration of the reactants and products are not necessarily equal to each other. For this to occur, the reaction must take place in a closed system in which none of the reactants or products can escape and in which no heat is added or lost.

Problem #1

Writing an Equilibrium Constant Expression from a Given Equilibrium Equation

Given the following equilibrium reaction: $aA + bB + \ldots \leftrightarrow cC + dD$, the equilibrium constant is calculated by the expression $k = \frac{[C]^c[D]^d}{[A]^a[B]^b}$. The brackets indicate "the concentration of" each individual reactant and product. The coefficients from the balanced chemical equation are used for the exponents in the equilibrium constant expression. Pure liquids and pure solids are not represented in the equilibrium constants. The concentration of gases and the concentration of solutes do appear in the expressions for equilibrium constants. Note that the concentrations of the products are in the numerator and the concentrations of the reactant are in the denominator.

Problem #2

Write equilibrium constant expressions for each of the following equilibriums:

1. $2SO_2(g) + O_2(g) \leftrightarrow 2SO_3(g)$.
2. $CaCO_3(s) \leftrightarrow CaO(s) + CO_2(g)$.
3. $CaH_2(s) + 2H_2O(l) \leftrightarrow Ca(OH)_2(aq) + 2H_2(g)$.
4. $H^+(aq) + OH^-(aq) \leftrightarrow H_2O(l)$.

1. All of the reactants and products are gases and need to be represented in the equilibrium constant. The concentration of the product is placed in the numerator, and the concentrations of the reactants are placed in the denominator. The coefficients from the balanced chemical equation are the exponents:

$$k = \frac{[SO_3]^2}{[SO_2]^2[O_2]}.$$

2. The solid reactant $CaCO_3$ and the solid product CaO are not part of the equilibrium constant. The concentration of the gaseous product CO_2 is represented in the numerator.

$$k = [CO_2].$$

3. The solid reactant CaH_2 and the liquid reactant H_2O are not part of the equilibrium constant. Both products should be represented. The "2" coefficient of the gaseous hydrogen is the exponent on the concentration of the gaseous H_2.

$$k = [Ca(OH)_2][H_2]^2.$$

4. Pure liquids are not represented in the equilibrium constant. Aqueous solutions are included in the equilibrium constant.

$$k = \frac{1}{[H^+][OH^-]}.$$

Le Châtelier's Principle

Le Châtelier's principle states that when a stressor is applied to a system in equilibrium, the system will respond in such a way to at least partially offset the stressor. Stressors include increasing or decreasing the temperature, increasing or decreasing the concentration of a reactant or product, and increasing or decreasing the pressure. Systems are described as "shifting left" or "shifting right" when a stressor is applied. For example, if the temperature is increased in an equilibrium in which the forward reaction is endothermic, the system will "shift right" in order to "use up" the heat that was applied. Increasing or decreasing the pressure of an equilibrium will only cause the equilibrium to "shift" if the number of moles of gases of the reactants differs from the number of moles of gases of the products. If there are no gases in the equilibrium or if the number of moles of gases of the reactants and products is equal, the change in pressure will have no effect on the equilibrium.

Example #1

Given the following equilibrium system, explain the effect of increasing the pressure on the production of ammonia:

$$3H_2(g) + N_2(g) \leftrightarrow 2NH_3(g) \Delta H = -92 \text{ kJ/mol}.$$

Le Châtelier's principle states that when a stressor is applied to a system in equilibrium, the system will respond in such a way to at least partially offset the stressor. An increase or decrease in pressure will only affect an equilibrium if the number of moles of gases of the reactants differs from the number of moles of gases of the products. In this equilibrium, the total number of moles of gases of the reactants of the forward reaction is 4 moles, and the number of moles of gases of the products of the forward reaction is 2 moles. To offset an increase in pressure, the equilibrium will "shift" to the side with the lesser number of moles of gases to relieve that pressure. This equilibrium "shifts right" or from 4 moles of gas to 2 moles of gas. When the equilibrium shifts right, the concentration of ammonia in the equilibrium increases, resulting in an increase in the production of ammonia.

Example #2

Given the following equilibrium system, explain the effect of increasing the temperature on the production of ammonia:

$$3H_2(g) + N_2(g) \leftrightarrow 2NH_3(g) \Delta H = -92 \text{ kJ/mol}.$$

Le Châtelier's principle states that when a stressor is applied to a system in equilibrium, the system will respond in such a way to at least partially offset the stressor. Because the forward reaction of the equilibrium is exothermic ($\Delta H < 0$), the reaction can be written as $3H_2(g) + N_2(g) \leftrightarrow 2NH_3(g)$ + heat. According to Le Châtelier's principle, the system will shift to offset or "use up" that heat. In this scenario, the equilibrium "shifts left." With a "shift to the left," more ammonia is "used up" as a reactant in the reverse reaction resulting in the overall production of ammonia decreasing.

Calculating K_{sp} and Percent Dissociation

The solubility product constant, K_{sp}, is the equilibrium constant for a solution equilibrium. If a general chemical equation for a solution equilibrium is given by ionic compound (s) ↔ cation (aq) + anion (aq), then the solubility product constant K_{sp} = [cation][anion]. The percent dissociation for each ion is calculated by the following formula: percent dissociation = $\frac{\text{amount dissociated}}{\text{initial concentration}} \times 100\ \%$, where the amount dissociated in the molarity of the ion in solution and the initial concentration is the molarity of the original compound. In general, the more dilute a solution, the greater the percent dissociation.

Calculate the Solubility of AgBr if the Solubility Product Constant, K_{sp}, for AgBr is 4.9×10^{-13} at 25 °C.

The dissociation reaction for AgBr can be written as:

$$AgBr(s) \leftrightarrow Ag^+(aq) + Br^-(aq).$$

Because the dissociation of AgBr produces equal moles of Ag^+ and Br^- ions, the solubility is simply the concentration of the Ag^+ ions, $[Ag^+]$, or the concentration of the Br^- ions, $[Br^-]$. The solubility product constant for this reaction is given by $K_{sp} = [Ag^+][Br^-]$, but because $[Ag^+] = [Br^-]$, this can be written as $K_{sp} = [Ag^+]^2$. Substituting in the given value for K_{sp} yields $4.9 \times 10^{-13} = [Ag^+]^2$. Therefore, $[Ag^-] = 7.0 \times 10^{-7}$ M. Finally, the solubility of AgBr is 7.0×10^{-7} M.

Solubility of Ionic Compounds in Water

If an ionic compound is soluble in water, the cations and anions will separate from each other when combined with water. In general, the rule for solubility is "like dissolves like." However, some ionic compounds are not soluble in water because the forces joining the ions are stronger than the intermolecular forces between the ions and the water molecules. Some general guidelines regarding solubility include the following: All nitrates and acetates are soluble. All chlorides, bromides, and iodides are soluble except those of silver, mercury(I), and lead(II). All sulfates are soluble except those of strontium, barium, mercury(I), and lead(II). All sulfides are insoluble except those of ammonium, the alkali metal cations, calcium, strontium, and barium. All carbonates are insoluble except those of ammonium and the alkali metal cations. All phosphates are insoluble except those of ammonium and the alkali metal cations. All hydroxides are insoluble except those of the alkali metal cations and calcium, strontium, and barium.

Soluble Ionic Compounds		**Important Exceptions**
Compounds containing	NO_3^-	None
	$C_2H_3O_2^-$	None
	Cl^-	Compounds of Ag^+, Hg_2^{2+}, and Pb^{2+}
	Br^-	Compounds of Ag^+, Hg_2^{2+}, and Pb^{2+}
	I^-	Compounds of Ag^+, Hg_2^{2+}, and Pb^{2+}
	SO_4^-	Compounds of Sr^{2+}, Ba^{2+}, Hg_2^{2+}, and Pb^{2+}
Insoluble Ionic Compounds		**Important Exceptions**
	S^{2-}	Compounds of NH_4^+, the alkali metal cations, and Ca^{2+}, Sr^{2+}, and Ba^{2+}
	CO_3^{2-}	Compounds of NH_4^+ and the alkali metal cations
	PO_4^{3-}	Compounds of NH_4^+ and the alkali metal cations
	OH^-	Compounds of the alkali metal cations, and Ca^{2+}, Sr^{2+}, and Ba^{2+}

Common Ion Effect

The common ion effect is the decrease in the solubility of a salt in an electrolyte when that electrolyte solution already has an ion in common with that salt. An example of the common ion effect is when sodium chloride, NaCl, is dissolved in an aqueous solution of hydrochloric acid, HCl. The ions of the NaCl are Na^+ and Cl^-, and the ions of the HCl solution are H^+ and Cl^-. Therefore, the solute NaCl and the aqueous solution HCl share a common Cl^- ion. The equilibrium of the aqueous HCl solution can be represented by the following equation:$HCl\ (s) + H_20\ (l) \leftrightarrow H_3O^+\ (aq) + Cl^-\ (aq)$.

According to Le Châtelier's principle, when a stressor is applied to this equilibrium, the system will respond in such a way to at least partially offset the stressor. Adding the NaCl to this equilibrium increases the concentration of the Cl^- ions in solution, which would shift to the equilibrium to the left. The overall effect is that less Cl^- goes into solution. Therefore, because the solute and the solution share a common ion, the common ion effect is shown as the decrease in the solubility of the Cl^- ions.

ELECTROLYTES AND NONELECTROLYTES

Electrolytes are substances that dissociate in solution to form ions. Strong electrolytes ionize essentially completely. Weak electrolytes only ionize partially and form only a few ions in solution. Nonelectrolytes do not dissociate or form ions in solution. Strong electrolytes such as salt water, NaCl (aq), or hydrochloric acid, HCl (aq), are good conductors of electricity. Weak electrolytes such as acetic acid, $HC_2H_2O_2$ (aq), and ammonia, NH_3 (aq), are poor conductors of electricity. Nonelectrolytes such as sugar water, $C_{12}H_{22}O_{11}$ (aq), and ethanol, C_2H_5OH (aq), do not conduct electricity.

Mathematical Analysis

Significant Figures

Significant figures enable scientists to determine which measurements are very precise and which measurements are not as precise. Every measurement has uncertainty. When recording data, the use of the correct number of significant figures indicates the precision of the equipment being used to measure the data. In general, measurements are recorded only to the first uncertain digit. This means that the final recorded digit is considered to be uncertain. Every calculated value using collected data has uncertainty. Significant figures determine where to round when doing calculations with data. Also, significant figures prevent the answers to calculations from being stated with higher precision than the data used in the calculation would actually support.

When using significant figures in calculations, there are two sets of rules: one for addition and subtraction, and one for multiplication and division. For addition and subtraction calculations, answers should be rounded to the leftmost uncertain digit. For example, when adding measurements of 2.3 g and 10.81 g, the correct answer would be 13.1 g. The first term's uncertain digit is in the tenths place, while the second term's uncertain digit is in the hundredths place. Thus, the answer is rounded to the tenths place. In multiplication and division calculations, answers should be rounded to the exact number of significant figures in the factor that has the smallest number of significant figures. For example, when multiplying 3.2 by 4.001, the correct answer may only have 2 significant figures because 3.2 only has 2 significant figures. Therefore, the correct answer is 13. If the first factor were instead 3.20 or 3.200 (indicating that this value was known with greater precision), the answer would be 12.8 or 12.80, respectively.

Problems

PERFORM THE FOLLOWING CALCULATIONS USING SIGNIFICANT FIGURES

1. 235.2008 + 304.02 + 467.9.
2. 1,303.69 – 1,245.
3. 400.0 × 2.3000.
4. 2.30/0.00040.

1. 235.2008 + 304.02 + 467.9.

   When adding numbers using significant figures, the answer should be rounded to the place that has the greatest uncertainty. For these addends, the number 467.9 has the greatest uncertainty in the tenths place. Therefore, the correct answer is 1,007.1.

2. 1,303.69 – 1,245.

   When subtracting numbers using significant figures, the answer should be rounded to the place that has the greatest uncertainty. In this problem, the number 1,245 has the greatest uncertainty in the ones place. Therefore, the correct answer is 59.

3. 400.0 × 2.3000.

   When multiplying numbers using significant figures, determine the number of significant figures in each factor. The number 400.0 has four significant figures, and the number 2.3000 has five significant figures. Therefore, the answer should contain only four significant figures. The correct answer is 920.0.

4. 2.30/0.00040.

When dividing numbers using significant figures, determine the number of significant figures in each number involved in the calculation. The number 2.30 has three significant figures, and the number 0.00040 has two significant figures. Therefore, the answer should have only two significant figures. The correct answer is 5,800.

Proper Organization and Presentation of Data

During a chemistry laboratory, all laboratory data should be collected in a lab notebook. All data should include the date and time collected. If possible, all data should be collected in structured tables. All appropriate raw data including units and uncertainties must be collected. The certain digits and the first uncertain or estimated digit should always be included. The raw data must be processed correctly. Calculations should be meticulous, keeping significant figures correct and units in order. Processed data should be presented in the form of graphs that highlight relationships, correlations, and trends. All graphs should have titles and be carefully labeled including the correct units. For example, scatterplots with lines of best fit could be used if the data show a linear relationship between variables.

Recognizing Trends

When reading tables, graphs, and charts, determine if there is a correlation between the data for the independent variable and the data for the dependent variable. The correlation is positive if both data sets increase together. The correlation is negative if one set of data increases while the other set of data decreases. If a scatterplot is drawn, determine if there is a positive correlation, a negative correlation, or no correlation between the variables. If a correlation is found, determine if the correlation is linear or curvilinear. If there is a linear correlation, a line of best fit can be drawn to make predictions. Graphing calculators can be used to perform linear regression of the data and determine the equation for the line of best fit. Use of linear regression will increase the accuracy of predictions.

Metric Units

Quantity	Name	Symbol
Mass	Kilogram	kg
Volume	Liter	L
Length	Meter	m
Time	Second	s
Absolute temperature	Kelvin	K
Amount of a substance	Mole	mole
Energy	Joule	J
Pressure	Pascal	Pa
Force	Newton	N
Frequency	Hertz	Hz
Electric current	Ampere	A
Luminous intensity	Candela	cd

Converting Milligrams to Kilograms and Kilograms to Milligrams

One kilogram is equal to 1,000 g. One gram is equal to 1,000 mg. One way to convert between these units is the dimensional analysis method using the conversion factors of $\left(\frac{1\text{ kg}}{1000\text{ g}}\right)$ and $\left(\frac{1\text{ g}}{1000\text{ mg}}\right)$. For example, convert 5,400 mg to kg by multiplying $(5{,}400\text{ mg})\left(\frac{1\text{ g}}{1000\text{ mg}}\right)\left(\frac{1\text{kg}}{1000\text{ g}}\right) = 5.4 \times 10^{-3}$ kg. To convert 7,200 kg to mg, multiply $(7{,}200\text{ kg})\left(\frac{1000\text{ g}}{\text{kg}}\right)\left(\frac{1000\text{ mg}}{\text{g}}\right) = 7.2 \times 10^{9}$ mg.

Converting to and from Degrees Fahrenheit, Degrees Celsius, and Kelvin

To convert from degrees Fahrenheit to degrees Celsius, use the formula $°C = \frac{5}{9}(°F - 32)$. To convert from degrees Celsius to degrees Fahrenheit, use the formula $°F = \frac{9}{5}°C + 32$. To convert from degrees Celsius to kelvin, use the formula K = °C + 273.15. To convert from kelvin to degrees Celsius, use the formula °C = K – 273.15. To convert from degrees Fahrenheit to kelvin, first convert the degrees Fahrenheit to degrees Celsius and then the degrees Celsius to kelvin. To convert from kelvin to degrees Fahrenheit, first convert the kelvin temperature to degrees Celsius and then convert the degrees Celsius to degrees Fahrenheit.

Conversion Problems

Perform each of the following conversions.

1. 250.0 mL to L
2. 0.050 mg to kg
3. 113 °F to K

1. 250.0 mL to L

Because 1 L contains 1,000 mL, the conversion factor is $\left(\frac{1\text{ L}}{1{,}000\text{ mL}}\right)$. Using dimensional analysis and multiplying, $(250.0\text{ mL})\left(\frac{1\text{ L}}{1{,}000\text{ mL}}\right) = 0.2500$ L.

2. 0.050 mg to kg

Because 1kg contains 1,000 g, and 1 g contains 1,000 mg, the conversion factors are $\left(\frac{1\text{ kg}}{1{,}000\text{ g}}\right)$ and $\left(\frac{1\text{ g}}{1000\text{ mg}}\right)$. Using dimensional analysis and multiplying, $(0.0500\text{ mg})\left(\frac{1\text{ g}}{1{,}000\text{ mg}}\right)\left(\frac{1\text{ kg}}{1{,}000\text{ g}}\right) = 5.00 \times 10^{-8}$ kg.

3. 113 °F to K

Substituting 113 °F into the formula $°C = \frac{5}{9}(°F - 32)$ yields $°C = \frac{5}{9}(113 - 32) = 45.0$ °C. Then, substituting 45.0 °C into the formula K = °C + 273.15 yields K = 45.0 + 273.15 = 273.2 K.

Scientific Notation

Scientific notation is a convenient way to write extremely large or extremely small numbers. Any rational number can be written in scientific notation. The format is $M \times 10^{n}$, where M is a number between 1 and 10 and n is a positive or negative integer. The first number (M) is called the coefficient, and the second number (10^{n}) is called the base. For numbers greater than 1, n is positive. For numbers less than 1, n is negative. For example, the number 6,200,000 is written as 6.2

$\times 10^6$, and the number 0.000047 is written as 4.7×10^{-5}. To convert from scientific notation, simply move the decimal point the same number of places as the exponent. Move the decimal to the right if the exponent is positive and to the left if the exponent is negative. For example, 3.1×10^4 is 31,000, and 8.6×10^{-3} is 0.0086.

Calculation Problems

Perform the Following Calculations.

1. $(4.00 \times 10^{-3})(5.00 \times 10^{-2})$
2. $(8.0 \times 10^4)/(4.0 \times 10^{-4})$
3. $(2.0 \times 10^3) + (4.1 \times 10^4)$
4. $(3.0 \times 10^{-5}) - (3.0 \times 10^{-6})$

1. $(4.00 \times 10^{-3})(5.00 \times 10^{-2})$

    To multiply numbers that are written in scientific notation, first multiply the coefficients. In this problem, (4.00)(5.00) = 20.0. Next, add the exponents. In this problem, (−3) + (−2) = −5. If the new coefficient had been less than 10, the calculation would be done. However, in this problem, combining the coefficient with the new base yields 20.0×10^{-5}, which is not written in correct scientific notation. When this occurs, move the decimal to the left until the coefficient is between 1 and 10 and then adjust the exponent accordingly. In this problem, the correct answer is 2.0×10^{-4}.

2. $(8.0 \times 10^4)/(4.0 \times 10^{-4})$

    To divide numbers that are written in scientific notation, divide the coefficients and subtract the exponents. In this problem, 8.0/4.0 = 2.0, and 4 − (−4) = 8. The correct answer is 2.0×10^8.

3. $(2.0 \times 10^3) + (4.1 \times 10^4)$

    To add numbers that are written in scientific notation, expand the numbers in order to line up the decimals. In this problem 2,000 + 41,000 = 43,000, which can be written in scientific notation as 4.3×10^4.

4. $(3.0 \times 10^{-5}) - (3.0 \times 10^{-6})$

    To subtract numbers that are written in scientific notation, expand the numbers in order to line up the decimals. In this problem, 0.000030 − 0.0000030 = 0.000027, which can be written in scientific notation as 2.7×10^{-5}.

Basic Measurement Equipment

Chemistry laboratories should be equipped with the following basic measurement equipment: triple-beam balances or digital balances for measuring mass, graduated cylinders for measuring volumes of liquids, graduated pipettes for measuring small volumes of liquids, thermometers for measuring temperature, pH meters for measuring pH, and rulers for measuring length. Manometers may also be used to measure the pressure of gases. Burettes may be used to measure volumes of acids or bases used in titrations. Viscometers may be used to determine the viscosity of liquids.

Problem

Calculate the mean of the following data: 2.300, 2.410, 2.210, 2.350, 2.300, 2.210.

The mean is the average of a group of data. To find the mean, find the sum of the data and then divide the sum by the number of data points. For example, to find the average of the data: 2.300, 2.410, 2.210, 2.350, 2.300, 2.210, first, find the sum of 2.300 + 2.410 + 2.210 + 2.350 + 2.300 + 2.210 = 13.78. Next, divide the sum of 13.78 by 6 because there are six data points. This yields 13.78/6 = 2.297.

Accuracy and Precision

Accuracy is the exactness of a measurement or how close a measurement is to the actual value. Precision is the consistency of a measurement or the repeatability of a measurement. For example, the figure on the left represents dart throwing that is neither precise nor accurate because there is no grouping of the darts nor are any darts close to the bull's-eye. The figure in the middle represents dart throwing that is precise due to the grouping of the darts but not accurate due to the location of the group. The figure on the right represents dart throwing that is precise and accurate due to the grouping of the darts and the location of the grouping near the bull's-eye.

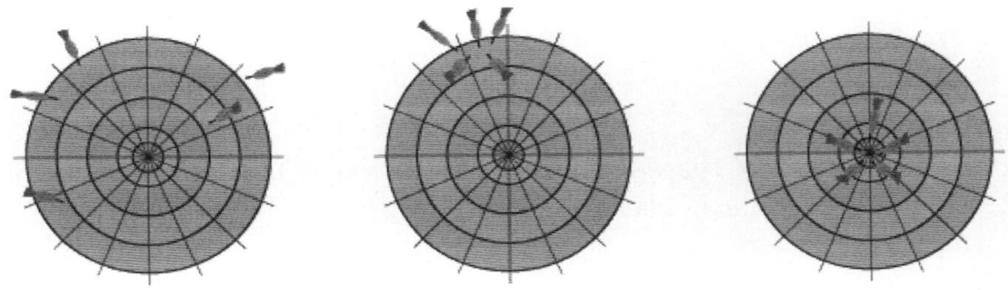

Given these data from two balances in a chemistry laboratory, explain how to determine which of the two balances is more accurate and more precise if the actual mass of the sample is 7.823 g.

Trial	Triple-Beam Balance	Digital Balance
1	7.81 g	7.824 g
2	7.82 g	7.823 g
3	7.80 g	7.824 g
4	7.80 g	7.823 g
5	7.81 g	7.824 g

In order to determine which balance is more accurate, find the range of differences of each measured value and the actual value for each balance. The range of differences for the triple-beam balance is between 0.003 and 0.023. The range of differences for the digital balance is between 0.000 and 0.001. Therefore, the digital balance is more accurate. In order to determine which balance is more precise, find the difference between the highest and lowest readings for each balance. The range of the data for the triple beam balance is 0.02. The range of the data for the digital balance is 0.001. Therefore, the digital balance is also more precise.

Random Error, Systematic Error, and Personal Error

Random error is also known as indeterminate error. Random errors are from unknown causes and are unpredictable. Systematic error is also known as determinate error. Systematic error is introduced into the data due to some defect in a procedure or an instrument that is faulty or not properly calibrated. For example, measurements that have errors due to imprecise tools are systematic errors. Systematic errors are difficult to detect and eliminate. Personal error is introduced into the data due to human mistakes. This would include the improper use of equipment, improperly following a procedure, and the incorrect reading of data. Personal error can often be minimized with proper training. Random error can cause random fluctuations in the data that are above or below the actual values. Systematic error will cause the data to be consistently high or consistently low. For example, a balance that is calibrated low by 0.01 g or a thermometer that is calibrated 3 °C low will each consistently provide low readings.

PERCENT ERROR

Percent error expresses the difference between the experimental value and the theoretical value (or actual value) and is written as a percent. To calculate percent error, subtract the theoretical value from the experimental value and divide the difference by the theoretical value. Then, multiply by 100 to convert this decimal to a percent. Finally, add a percent sign. If the situation is not appropriate to use a negative percent, then take the absolute value of the numerator before dividing:

$$\text{percent error} = \frac{\text{experimental value} - \text{theoretical value}}{\text{theoretical value}} \times 100\ \%.$$

EXAMPLE

In a laboratory experiment, the specific heat of a sample of copper is calculated to be 0.40 J/(g·°C). The actual specific heat of copper is 0.38 J/(g·°C). Explain how to calculate the percent error.

The percent error in the specific heat calculation can be calculated using the following formula:

$$\text{percent error} = \frac{\text{experimental value} - \text{theoretical value}}{\text{theoretical value}} \times 100\ \%.$$

Substituting in 0.40 J/(g·°C) for the experimental value and 0.38 J/(g·°C) in for the theoretical value yields the following: percent error $= \frac{0.40\ \text{J/(g·°C)} - 0.38\ \text{J/(g·°C)}}{0.38\ \text{J/(g·°C)}} \times 100\ \% = 5.3\ \%$. Note that the theoretical value is in the denominator. Also, after performing the division, the answer is in decimal form. Multiply by 100 to change the decimal to a percent, and then add the percent symbol.

Moles/Stoichiometry

LAW OF CONSERVATION OF ENERGY

The law of conservation of energy states that in a closed system, energy cannot be created or destroyed but only changed from one form to another. This is also known as the first law of thermodynamics. Another way to state this is that the total energy in an isolated system is constant. Energy comes in many forms that may be transformed from one kind to another, but in a closed system, the total amount of energy is conserved or remains constant. For example, potential energy can be converted in kinetic energy, thermal energy, radiant energy, or mechanical energy. In an isolated chemical reaction, there can be no energy created or destroyed. The energy simply changes forms.

LAW OF CONSERVATION OF MASS

The law of conservation of mass is also known as the law of conservation of matter. This basically means that in a closed system, the total mass of the products must equal the total mass of the reactants. This could also be stated that in a closed system, mass never changes. A consequence of this law is that matter is never created or destroyed during a typical chemical reaction. The atoms of the reactants are simply rearranged to form the products. The number and type of each specific atom involved in the reactants is identical to the number and type of atoms in the products. This is the key principle used when balancing chemical equations. In a balanced chemical equation, the number of moles of each element on the reactant side equals the number of moles of each element on the product side.

NAMING PROCESS FOR BINARY MOLECULAR COMPOUNDS

The names of binary molecular compounds follow this pattern:

prefix + first element name (space) prefix + root of second element name + -ide.

If a prefix ends with *a* or *o* and the element name begins with *a* or *o*, the first *a* or *o* of the prefix is dropped. For example, N_2O_5 is named dinitrogen pentoxide. The prefix *mono-* is usually dropped unless more than one binary compound may be formed from the two elements involved.

Binary Molecular Compounds

#	Prefix	#	Prefix
1	mono-	6	hexa-
2	di-	7	hepta-
3	tri-	8	octa-
4	tetra-	9	nona-
5	penta-	10	deca-

NAMING PROCESS FOR BINARY IONIC COMPOUNDS

The names of binary ionic compounds follow this pattern:

cation name (space) anion name.

The name of simple cations is usually the element name. For example, the K^+ cation is named potassium. Some cations exist in more than one form. In those cases, the charge of the ion follows the element as a Roman numeral in parentheses. For example, the Cu^+ ion is named copper(I) and the Cu^{2+} ion is named copper(II). Simple anions are named with the root of the element name followed by the suffix *-ide.* For example, the O^{2-} anion is named oxide, and the F^- ion is named fluoride. The following are some examples of names of binary ionic compounds: KI is named potassium iodide, and FeO is named iron(II) oxide.

EXAMPLES

N_2O_4 — This is a binary molecular compound. Using the prefixes *di-* for 2 and *tetra-* for 4, this compound is named dinitrogen tetroxide. Note that the entire element name is retained for the cation, but the root plus *-ide* is used for the anion name.

S_2F_{10} — This is a binary molecular compound. Using the prefixes *di-* for 2 and *deca-* for 10, this compound is named disulfur decafluoride. Note that the entire element name is retained for the cation, but the root plus *-ide* is used for the anion name.

Fe_2O_3 — This is a binary ionic compound. Iron forms two types of cations Fe^{2+} and Fe^{3+}, but because the anion is O^{2-}, this must be the Fe^{3+} ion in order to balance the charges. This compound is named iron(III) oxide.

$CuCl_2$ — This is a binary ionic compound. Copper forms two types of cations Cu^+ and Cu^{2+}, but because the anion is Cl^-, this must be the Cu^{2+} ion in order to balance the charges. This compound is named copper(II) chloride.

NAMING ACIDS

Acids are generally categorized as binary acids or oxyacids. Binary acids are named by the pattern: *hydro-* + root of element + *-ic* (space) acid. For example, HI is named hydroiodic acid, and HCl is named hydrochloric acid. One exception is that in hydrosulfuric acid (H_2S), the entire element name sulfur is used. The names of oxyacids depend on the endings of their polyatomic anions. If the polyatomic anions end in *-ate*, then the acid names end in *-ic*. If the anions end in *-ite*, the acid names end in *-ous*. The naming pattern for an oxyacid is as follows: anion root + ending (space) acid. For example, H_2CO_3 is named carbonic acid because the carbonate ion ends in *-ate*, and H_2SO_3 is named sulfurous acid because the sulfite ion ends in *-ite.*

NAMING BASES AND SALTS

Bases typically are ionic compounds with the hydroxide anion and are named following the conventions of naming ionic compounds. For example, NaOH is named sodium hydroxide and $Mg(OH)_2$ is named magnesium hydroxide. Salts are ionic compounds with any cation except H^+ from an aqueous base and any anion except OH^- from an aqueous acid. Salts are named like regular ionic compounds with the name of the cation followed by the name of the anion. Examples of salts include sodium chloride (NaCl), potassium fluoride (KF), magnesium iodide (MgI_2), sodium acetate ($NaC_2H_3O_2$), and ammonium carbonate ($(NH_4)_2CO_3$).

NAMING HYDRATES

Hydrates form from salts (ionic compounds) that attract water. Hydrates are named from their salt (ionic compound) name and the number of water molecules involved in the following pattern:

salt name (space) prefix + hydrate. For example, the name of $CuSO_4 \cdot 5H_2O$ is copper(II) sulfate pentahydrate, and the name of $CoCl_2 \cdot 6H_2O$ is cobalt(II) chloride hexahydrate.

Binary Molecular Compounds

#	Prefix	#	Prefix
1	mono-	6	hexa-
2	di-	7	hepta-
3	tri-	8	octa-
4	tetra-	9	nona-
5	penta-	10	deca-

AVOGADRO'S NUMBER, MOLAR MASS, AND THE MOLE

Avogadro's number is equivalent to the number of atoms in 12 g of the carbon-12 isotope or the number of atoms in 1 mole of carbon-12. Avogadro's number is numerically equal to approximately 6.022×10^{23}. Just like a dozen eggs represents 12 eggs and a pair of shoes represents 2 shoes, Avogadro's number of atoms represents 6.022×10^{23} atoms. *Molar mass* is the mass of one mole of a substance in grams. The *mole* is Avogadro's number of anything. For example, 1 mole of carbon atoms is 6.022×10^{23} carbon atoms, and 1 mole of CCl_4 contains 6.022×10^{23} molecules of CCl_4.

PROBLEM #1

DETERMINE THE MASS OF 2.50 MOLES OF O_2. (THE ATOMIC MASS OF OXYGEN IS 16.0 U.)

To convert from moles of O_2 to mass in grams of O_2, use the dimensional analysis method with the molar mass of O_2. The molar mass of O_2 is 2(16.0 g) or 32.0 g. This molar mass can be written as the conversion factor $(\frac{32.0 \text{ g } O_2}{\text{mol } O_2})$. Then, using dimensional analysis, multiply $(2.50 \text{ mol } O_2)(\frac{32.0 \text{ g } O_2}{\text{mol } O_2})$. The "mol O_2" cancels from the numerator of the first factor and the denominator of the second factor resulting in 80.0 g O_2.

PROBLEM #2

DETERMINE THE NUMBER OF MOLES OF 100.0 G OF $C_{12}H_{22}O_{11}$. (THE ATOMIC MASSES OF C, H, AND O ARE 12.0 U, 1.0 U, AND 16.0 U, RESPECTIVELY.)

To find the number of moles of a sample of $C_{12}H_{22}O_{11}$, first, calculate the molar mass to be used in dimensional analysis. The molar mass of $C_{12}H_{22}O_{11}$ = 12(12.0 g) + 22(1.0 g) + 11(16.0 g) = 144.0 g + 22.0 g + 176.0 g = 342 g. This means that every mole of $C_{12}H_{22}O_{11}$ has a molar mass of 342 g. To convert from grams to moles, use dimensional analysis as follows: $(100.0 \text{ g } C_{12}H_{22}O_{11})\left(\frac{1 \text{ mol } C_{12}H_{22}O_{11}}{342 \text{ g}}\right) = 0.292 \text{ mol}$.

PROBLEM #3

GIVEN THE REACTION $3H_2(g) + N_2(g) \rightarrow 2NH_3(g)$, EXPLAIN HOW TO DETERMINE HOW MANY GRAMS OF NITROGEN GAS ARE NEEDED TO PRODUCE 100.0 G OF AMMONIA. (THE MOLAR MASS OF N_2 = 28.0 G; THE MOLAR MASS OF NH_3 = 17.0 G.)

One approach to working out this problem is to use the dimensional analysis method all the way through the work of the problem. Conversion factors using the molar masses of NH_3 and N_2 are used as well as a mole ratio from the balanced chemical equation. The approach is to convert from grams of NH_3 to moles of NH_3, then to convert moles of NH_3 to moles of N_2, and finally to convert the moles of N_2 to grams of N_2.

$$\left(\frac{100.0\text{ g }NH_3}{1}\right)\left(\frac{1\text{ mol }NH_3}{17.0\text{ g}}\right)\left(\frac{1\text{ mol }N_2}{2\text{ mol }NH_3}\right)\left(\frac{28.0\text{ g }N_2}{1\text{ mol }N_2}\right) = 82.4\text{ g }N_2.$$

Finding an Empirical Formula and a Molecular Formula of a Compound

To find the empirical formula of a compound, first, calculate the masses of each element in the compound based on the percent composition that is given. Then, convert these masses to moles by dividing by the molar masses of those elements. Next, divide these amounts in moles by the smallest calculated value in moles and round to the nearest tenth. These calculations provide the subscripts for each element in the empirical formula. To find the molecular formula, divide the actual molar mass of the compound by the molar mass of the empirical formula.

Example

Find the empirical formula and the molecular formula for hydrogen peroxide given that it has a composition of 5.94 % hydrogen and 94.1 % oxygen. (The atomic mass for hydrogen = 1.008 u; the atomic mass of oxygen = 16.00 u.)

To find the empirical formula, calculate the masses of each element in hydrogen peroxide for a sample size of 100.0 g. Calculating 5.94 % of 100.0 g yields 5.94 g of hydrogen. Calculating 94.1 % of 100.0 g yields 94.1 g of oxygen. Next, convert the masses of these elements to moles. Multiplying (5.94 g hydrogen) $\left(\frac{\text{mol hydrogen}}{1.008\text{ g}}\right) =$ 5.89 mol hydrogen. Multiplying (94.1 g oxygen) $\left(\frac{\text{mol oxygen}}{16.00\text{ g}}\right) = 5.88$ mol oxygen. Now, divide these amounts by the smallest value of moles that was calculated and round to the nearest tenth. For hydrogen, $\left(\frac{5.89}{5.88}\right) = 1.0$, and for oxygen, $\left(\frac{5.88}{5.88}\right) = 1.0$. These calculations are the subscripts for the empirical formula. Therefore, the empirical formula of hydrogen peroxide is HO. To find the molecular formula, find the molar mass of the empirical formula (HO) by adding 1.008 g + 16.00 g = 17.008 g. To perform the calculation, the molar mass of hydrogen peroxide would need to be given. If the problem states that the actual molar mass of hydrogen peroxide is 34.016 g, divide this molar mass by the molar mass of the empirical formula: $\frac{34.016}{17.008} =$ 2. Multiply each subscript of the empirical formula by 2. The molecular formula for hydrogen peroxide is H_2O_2.

Calculating Percent Composition When Given the Molecular Formula

To find the percent composition when given the molecular formula, first find the molar mass of the compound. Next, find the percent contributed by each element of the compound by dividing the molar mass of the element (remembering to multiply through by the subscripts of the molecular formula) by the molar mass of the compound. Finally, check the calculations by totaling these individual percents of the elements to ensure their combined total is 100 %. This may be slightly off if any of the numbers used were rounded.

EXAMPLE

FIND THE PERCENT COMPOSITION OF METHANE (CH_4). (THE ATOMIC MASS OF CARBON = 12.01 U; THE ATOMIC MASS OF HYDROGEN = 1.008 U.)

To find the percent composition of methane, first find the molar mass of methane. The molar mass of methane is given by 12.01 g + 4(1.008 g) = 16.042 g. Next, find the percent contributed by the carbon and the percent contributed by the hydrogen. For the carbon, % C = $\frac{12.01\text{ g/mol}}{16.042\text{ g/mol}} \times 100\,\% = 74.87\,\%$. For the hydrogen, % H = $\frac{4(1.008)\text{ g/mol}}{16.042\text{ g/mol}} \times 100\,\% = 25.13\,\%$.Finally, check to see that the total of the calculated percents is 100 %. There may be a slight difference due to rounding. For methane, 74.87% + 25.13 % = 100%.

BALANCING A CHEMICAL EQUATION

According to the law of conservation of mass, the mass of the products must always equal the mass of the reactants in a chemical reaction. Because mass is conserved, the number of each type of atom in the products must equal the number of each type of atom in the reactants. The key to balancing a chemical reaction is in balancing the number of each type of atom on both sides of the equation. Only the coefficients in front of the reactants and products may be changed to accomplish this, not the subscripts in the molecules themselves. Try balancing the largest number of a type of atom first. Also, check if any odd numbers need to be changed to even. Always leave the uncombined elements to balance until the end.

EXAMPLE #1

Balance the equation $KNO_3(s) \rightarrow KNO_2(s) + O_2(g)$.

First, determine the types and numbers of each type of atom on each side of the equation:

Reactants		Products	
K	1	K	1
N	1	N	1
O	3	O	4

"Oxygen" needs to be balanced. Add a coefficient of "2" to the left side to force "oxygen" to be even and update the counts:

Reactants		Products	
K	2	K	1
N	2	N	1
O	6	O	4

Now, balance the potassium and nitrogen by placing a coefficient of "2" in front of the KNO_2 and update the counts:

Reactants		Products	
K	2	K	2
N	2	N	2
O	6	O	6

The equation is now balanced: $2KNO_3(s) \rightarrow 2KNO_2(s) + O_2(g)$.

EXAMPLE #2

Balance the equation $C_2H_2(g) + O_2(g) \rightarrow CO_2(g) + H_2O(g)$.

First, determine the types and numbers of each type of atom on each side of the equation:

Reactants		**Products**	
C	2	C	1
H	2	H	2
O	2	O	3

"Oxygen" needs to be balanced, but remember to leave the uncombined oxygen reactant until the end. "Carbon" also needs to be balanced. Add a coefficient of "4" to the CO_2 on the right side and a coefficient of "2" in front of the C_2H_2 and update the counts:

Reactants		**Products**	
C	4	C	4
H	4	H	2
O	2	O	9

Balance the "hydrogen" by adding a "2" in front of the H_2O and update the counts:

Reactants		**Products**	
C	4	C	4
H	4	H	4
O	2	O	10

Finally, balance the "oxygen" by adding a "5" in front of the O_2 on the left.

The equation is now balanced: $2C_2H_2\,(g) + 5O_2\,(g) \rightarrow 4CO_2\,(g) + 2H_2O\,(g)$.

BALANCED CHEMICAL EQUATION INVOLVING A SIMPLE OXIDATION-REDUCTION REACTION

One method to balance simple oxidation-reduction reactions is to split the reaction into half-reactions. First, write the oxidation half-reaction and the reduction half-reaction. Remember the phrase *"LEO the lion says GER,"* which is a reminder that the loss of electrons is oxidation, and the gain of electrons is reduction. Next, balance the electrons by multiply the equation(s) by the necessary factor(s). Finally, cancel the electron(s) and combine the balanced oxidation and reduction half-reactions into a balanced net chemical equation.

EXAMPLE #1

Balance the following chemical equation involving an oxidation-reduction reaction: $Na + O_2 \rightarrow Na^+ + O^{2-}$.

In order to balance the equation $Na + O_2 \rightarrow Na^+ + O^{2-}$, first, write the individual half-reactions:

oxidation: $Na \rightarrow Na^+ + e^-$

reduction: $O_2 + 4e^- \rightarrow 2O^{2-}$.

Next, balance the number of electrons by multiplying the oxidation half-reaction by 4:

oxidation: $4Na \rightarrow 4Na^+ + 4e^-$

reduction: $O_2 + 4e^- \rightarrow 2O^{2-}$.

Finally, cancel the electrons and combine the half-reactions into the net reaction:

$4Na + O_2 \rightarrow 4Na^+ + 2O^{2-}$.

EXAMPLE #2

GIVEN THE FOLLOWING EQUATION AT STANDARD TEMPERATURE AND PRESSURE (STP),

$4Fe\ (s) + 3O_2\ (g) \rightarrow 2Fe_2O_3\ (s)$, explain how to determine the volume of O_2 (g) needed to produce 10.0 moles of Fe_2O_3 (s).

One method to determine the volume of O_2 (g) needed to produce 10.0 moles of Fe_2O_3 (s) is to use dimensional analysis with the mole ratio for the balanced chemical equation. Because 3 moles of O_2 (g) produce 2 moles of Fe_2O_3 (s), the needed mole ratio is $\left(\frac{3 \text{ moles } O_2}{2 \text{ moles } Fe_2O_3}\right)$. Also, at STP, one mole of a gas has a volume of 22.4 L. This can be written as a conversion factor of $\left(\frac{22.4 \text{ L}}{1 \text{ mole } O_2}\right)$. Using dimensional analysis, $(10.0 \text{ mol } Fe_2O_3)\left(\frac{3 \text{ moles } O_2}{2 \text{ moles } Fe_2O_3}\right)\left(\frac{22.4 \text{ L}}{1 \text{ mole } O_2}\right) = 336 \text{ L}$.

Example #3

Given the following equation at STP,

C_3H_8 (l) + $5O_2$ (g) → $3CO_2$ (g)+ $4H_20$ (g),explain how to determine the volume of O_2 (g) needed to burn 1.00 kg of C_3H_8 (l).

One method to determine the volume of O_2 (g) needed to burn 1.0 kg of C_3H_8 (l) is to use dimensional analysis with conversion factors for the molar mass, number of moles, and liters of gas at STP. The conversion factor for the molar mass of C_3H_8 can be written as $\left(\frac{1 \text{ mol } C_3H_8}{44.1 \text{ grams } C_3H_8}\right)$. Because 1 mole of C_3H_8 (l) requires 5 moles of O_2 (g), the needed mole ratio is $\left(\frac{5 \text{ moles } O_2}{1 \text{ mole } C_3H_8}\right)$. Also, at STP, one mole of a gas has a volume of 22.4 L. This can be written as the conversion factor $\left(\frac{22.4 \text{ L}}{1 \text{ mole } O_2}\right)$. Using dimensional analysis, (1.0 kg of C_3H_8)$\left(\frac{1000 \text{ g}}{1 \text{ kg}}\right)\left(\frac{1 \text{ mole } C_3H_8}{44.1 \text{ g } C_3H_8}\right)\left(\frac{5 \text{ moles } O_2}{1 \text{ mole } C_3H_8}\right)\left(\frac{22.4 \text{ L } O_2}{1 \text{ mole } O_2}\right)$ = 2.54×10^3 L O_2.

Example #4

Given the following equation,

2Na (s) + Cl_2 (g) → 2NaCl (s), explain how to determine the amount in grams of Na (s) needed to produce 500.0 g of NaCl (s).

One method to determine the amount in grams of Na (s) needed to produce 500.0 g of NaCl (s) is to use dimensional analysis with conversion factors for the molar mass and number of moles. The conversion factor for the molar mass of NaCl (s) can be written as $\left(\frac{1 \text{ mol NaCl}}{58.44 \text{ g NaCl}}\right)$. Because 2 moles of Na (s) produce 2 moles of NaCl (s), the needed mole ratio is $\left(\frac{2 \text{ moles Na}}{2 \text{ moles NaCl}}\right)$. The conversion factor for the molar mass of Na can be written as $\left(\frac{22.99 \text{ g Na}}{1 \text{ mole Na}}\right)$. Using dimensional analysis, (500.0 g NaCl)$\left(\frac{1 \text{ mol NaCl}}{58.44 \text{ g NaCl}}\right)\left(\frac{2 \text{ moles Na}}{2 \text{ moles NaCl}}\right)\left(\frac{22.99 \text{ g Na}}{1 \text{ mole Na}}\right)$ = 196.7 g Na.

Example #5

Given the following equation at STP,

$2Na\ (s) + Cl_2\ (g) \rightarrow 2NaCl\ (s)$, explain how to determine the volume of Cl_2 (g) needed to produce 1.00 kg of NaCl(s).

One method to determine the volume of Cl_2 (g) needed to produce 1.00 kg of NaCl (s) is to use dimensional analysis with conversion factors for the molar mass, number of moles, and liters of gas at STP. The conversion factor for the molar mass of NaCl can be written as $\left(\frac{1\text{ mol NaCl}}{58.44\text{ g NaCl}}\right)$. Because 1 mole of Cl_2 (g) produces 2 moles of NaCl (s), the needed mole ratio is $\left(\frac{1\text{ mole }Cl_2}{2\ mole\ NaCl}\right)$. Also, at STP, one mole of a gas has a volume of 22.4 L. This can be written as a conversion factor $\left(\frac{22.4\text{ L}}{1\text{ mole }Cl_2}\right)$. Using dimensional analysis, $(1.00\text{ kg NaCl})\left(\frac{1000\text{ g}}{1\text{ kg}}\right)\left(\frac{1\text{ mol NaCl}}{58.44\text{ g NaCl}}\right)\left(\frac{1\text{ mole }Cl_2}{2\ mole\ NaCl}\right)\left(\frac{22.4\text{ L }O_2}{1\text{ mole }O_2}\right) =$ 191.65 L Cl_2, which rounds up to 192 L because 191 L will not be enough.

Limiting Reagent

The limiting reagent, or limiting reactant, is the reactant that determines or "limits" the amount of product formed. The limiting reagent is totally consumed in the chemical reaction. The other reactants in the chemical reaction must be present in excess amounts than what is needed. The excess reactants will be left over after the limiting reactant is consumed. To determine the limiting reagent from the balanced chemical equation, select one of the products and calculate how much of that product can be produced from each reactant. The reactant that produces the least amount of that product is the limiting reactant or limiting reagent.

Calculating the Percent Yield for a Chemical Reaction

To calculate the percent yield for a chemical reaction, use the formula:

$$\text{percent yield} = \frac{\text{actual yield}}{\text{theoretical yield}} \times 100\ \%.$$

The actual yield should be stated in the problem or determined experimentally. The theoretical yield can be calculated from the balanced chemical equation with dimensional analysis using conversion factors for molar mass and number of moles. Divide the actual yield by the theoretical yield. This is a decimal that can be converted to a percent by multiplying by 100 and adding the percent sign.

Example #1

Given that 100.0 g of H_2 (g) react with 350.0 g of O_2 (g), explain how to determine the limiting reactant and the amount of excess reactant that remains.

$2H_2\ (g) + O_2\ (g) \rightarrow 2H_2O\ (g)$.

To determine the limiting reactant, first determine the amount of H_2O that can be produced from each of the reactants:

- $(100.0\text{ g }H_2)\left(\frac{1\text{ mole }H_2}{2.016\text{ g }H_2}\right)\left(\frac{2\text{ moles }H_2O}{2\text{ moles }H_2}\right)\left(\frac{18.016\text{ g }H_2O}{1\text{ mole }H_2O}\right) = 893.7\text{ g }H_2O.$
- $(350.0\text{ g }O_2)\left(\frac{1\text{ mole }O_2}{32.00\text{ g }O_2}\right)\left(\frac{2\text{ moles }H_2O}{1\text{ mole }O_2}\right)\left(\frac{18.016\text{ g }H_2O}{1\text{ mole }H_2O}\right) = 394.1\text{ g }H_2O.$

Because O_2 produces the least amount of H_2O, O_2 is the limiting reagent. Therefore, H_2 is the reactant that is in excess. Calculating the amount of H_2 consumed in this reaction:

$$(350.0 \text{ g } O_2)\left(\frac{1 \text{ mole } O_2}{32.00 \text{ g } O_2}\right)\left(\frac{2 \text{ moles } H_2}{1 \text{ mole } O_2}\right)\left(\frac{2.016 \text{ g } H_2}{1 \text{ mole } H_2}\right) = 44.10 \text{ g } H_2 \text{ (consumed)}.$$

Subtracting this amount from the original amount yields the excess amount: 100.0 g H_2 – 44.10 g H_2 = 55.91 g H_2 (excess).

Example #2

Find the percent yield in the following reaction if 200.0 g of solid $KClO_3$ produced 100.0 g of solid KCl.

$2KClO_3\,(s) \rightarrow 2KCl\,(s) + 3O_2\,(g)$.

To calculate the percent yield if 200.0 g of solid $KClO_3$ produced 100.0 g of solid KCl, first calculate the theoretical yield of KCl or the maximum amount of KCl that can be produced.

Theoretical yield:

$$(200.0 \text{ g } KClO_3)\left(\frac{1 \text{ mole } KClO_3}{122.6 \text{ g } KClO_3}\right)\left(\frac{2 \text{ moles KCl}}{2 \text{ moles } KClO_3}\right)\left(\frac{74.55 \text{ g KCl}}{1 \text{ mole KCl}}\right) = 121.6 \text{ g KCl}.$$

The formula to calculate percent yield is percent yield = $\frac{\text{actual yield}}{\text{theoretical yield}} \times 100\,\%$. Substituting in the 100.0 g of KCl for the actual yield and the 121.6 g of KCl for the theoretical yield,

$$\text{percent yield} = \frac{100.0 \text{ g}}{121.6 \text{ g}} \times 100\,\% = 82.24\,\%.$$

Example #3

Balanced Equation for the Combustion of Methane

The molecular formula for methane is CH_4. For a combustion equation, the reactants are methane (CH_4) and oxygen gas (O_2). The products of this combustion reaction are water vapor (H_2O) and carbon dioxide (CO_2). Setting up the equation yields the following reaction:

$CH_4\,(g) + O_2\,(g) \rightarrow CO_2\,(g) + H_2O\,(g)$.

This equation must still be balanced. Finally, the combustion of methane is given by the following reaction:

$CH_4\,(g) + 2O_2\,(g) \rightarrow CO_2\,(g) + 2H_2O\,(g)$.

Example #4

Balanced Equation for the Neutralization of Hydrochloric Acid, HCl (aq), with Sodium Hydroxide, NaOH (aq)

In a neutralization reaction, an acid reacts with a base to form a salt and water. The salt forms from the cation of the base and the anion of the acid. The salt formed from these reactants is NaCl with the Na^+ from the base and the Cl^- from the acid. Water forms from the remaining H^+ and OH^- ions:

acid + base → salt + water

$HCl\ (aq) + NaOH\ (aq) \rightarrow NaCl\ (aq) + H_2O\ (l)$.

Example #5

Balanced Equation for the Decomposition Reaction of Solid Lithium Carbonate (Li_2CO_3)

The general form for a decomposition reaction is AB → A + B. However, this metal oxide has three elements and may at first not seem to fit the general form. When many metal carbonates are heated, they form the metal oxide and carbon dioxide gas. In this case, the products will also be compounds. In this decomposition reaction, when heated, solid lithium oxide decomposes to form solid lithium oxide and gaseous carbon dioxide:

$Li_2CO_3(s) \xrightarrow{\Delta} LiO(s) + CO_2(g)$.

Example #6

Balanced Equation for the Dehydration of Ethanol

Ethanol (C2H5OH) can be dehydrated to produce ethene (C_2H_4). The gaseous ethanol is passed over a hot aluminum oxide catalyst to produce ethene and water.

$\text{ethanol} \xrightarrow{\text{aluminum oxide}} \text{ethene} + \text{water}$

$C_2H_5OH\ (g) \xrightarrow{Al_2O_3} C_2H_4\ (g) + H_2O\ (l)$.

This can also be shown in the form of condensed structural formulas:

$CH_3CH_2OH \xrightarrow{Al_2O_3} CH_2 = CH_2 + H_2O$.

Single- and Double-Replacement Reactions

Single-replacement reactions, which are also known as single-displacement reactions or substitution reactions, have the general form of A + BC → AC + B. An example of a single-replacement reaction is the displacement of hydrogen from hydrochloric acid by zinc metal as given in the following equation:

$Zn\ (s) + 2HCl\ (aq) \rightarrow ZnCl_2\ (aq) + H_2\ (aq)$.

Double-replacement reactions, which are also known as double-displacement reactions, have the general form of AB + CD → AD + CB. An example of a double-replacement reaction is when aqueous solutions of lead(II) nitrate and potassium iodide react to form solid lead(II) iodide and aqueous potassium nitrate as given by the following equation:

$Pb(NO_3)_2\ (aq) + 2KI\ (aq) \rightarrow PbI_2\ (s) + 2KNO_3\ (aq)$.

Example #7

Identify Each Reaction Type as a Single- or Double-Replacement Reaction, and Predict the Products of the Following Equations:

1. $Mg\ (s) + 2\ H_2O\ (l) \rightarrow$.

2. $Pb(NO_3)_2$ (aq) + 2 KI (aq) →.

1. This reaction must be a single-replacement reaction because the left side corresponds to the left side of the general equation A + BC → AB + C. In this case, the magnesium replaces some of the hydrogen, and the products are hydrogen gas and magnesium hydroxide.

Mg (s) + $2H_2O$ (l) → $Mg(OH)_2$ (aq) + H_2 (g).

2. This reaction must be a double-replacement reaction because the left side corresponds to the left side of the general equation AB + CD → AD + CB. In this case, the Pb^+ cation from the $Pb(NO_3)_2$ bonds with the I^- anion from the KI to form solid PbI_2. The NO_3^- anion from the $Pb(NO_3)_2$ bonds with the K^+ cation from the KI to form aqueous KNO_3. $Pb(NO_3)_2$ (aq) + 2KI (aq) → PbI_2 (s) + $2KNO_3$ (aq).

EXAMPLE #8

BALANCED EQUATION FOR THE OXIDATION-REDUCTION REACTION OF METALLIC ZINC POWDER AND AQUEOUS COPPER(II) SULFATE

According to the activity series, zinc is more reactive than copper. Therefore, the zinc is oxidized, and the copper is reduced. Write the half-reactions:

oxidation: $Zn \rightarrow Zn^{2+} + 2e^-$.

reduction: $Cu^{2+} + 2e^- \rightarrow Cu$.

Cancel the electrons and combine the two half-reactions into the net equation:

$Zn + Cu^{2+} \rightarrow Zn^{2+} + Cu$.

Finally, add the symbols to indicate the state of each reactant and product:

Zn (s) + Cu^{2+} (aq) → Zn^{2+} (aq) + Cu (s).

Interestingly, this equation can also be written as the following single-displacement reaction:

Zn (s) + $CuSO_4$ (aq) → $ZnSO_4$ (aq) + Cu (s).

This single-displacement reaction has the same net ionic equation after canceling out the spectator ions.

EXAMPLE #9

BALANCED EQUATION FOR THE OXIDATION-REDUCTION REACTION OF A PIECE OF SOLID COPPER WIRE IMMERSED IN AN AQUEOUS SOLUTION OF SILVER NITRATE

According to the activity series, copper is more reactive than silver. Therefore, the copper is oxidized, and the silver is reduced. Write the half-reactions:

oxidation: $Cu \rightarrow Cu^{2+} + 2e^-$.

reduction: $Ag^+ + e^- \rightarrow Ag$.

Multiply the reduction half-reaction by 2 to balance the number of electrons:

oxidation: $Cu \rightarrow Cu^{2+} + 2e^{-}$.

reduction: $2Ag^{+} + 2e^{-} \rightarrow 2Ag$.

Cancel the electrons and combine the two half-reactions into the net equation:

$Cu + 2Ag^{+} \rightarrow Cu^{2+} + 2Ag$.

Finally, add the symbols to indicate the state of each reactant and product:

$Cu\ (s) + 2Ag^{+}\ (aq) \rightarrow Cu^{2+}\ (aq) + 2Ag\ (s)$.

Note that this equation is also classified as a single-displacement reaction:

$Cu\ (s) + 2AgNO_3\ (aq) \rightarrow Cu(NO_3)_2\ (aq) + 2Ag\ (s)$.

This single-displacement reaction has the same net ionic equation after canceling out the spectator ions.

Nuclear Chemistry

Alpha Particles

Alpha particles are the products of alpha decay. They are identical to helium nuclei. Alpha particles consist of two protons and two neutrons. Because they have two protons but zero electrons, alpha particles have a net +2 charge. They are represented by the Greek letter alpha as α, α^{2+}, or ${}^{4}_{2}\alpha^{2+}$. Because they are identical to helium nuclei, they may also be written as He^{2+}, ${}^{4}_{2}He$, or ${}^{4}_{2}He^{2+}$. Because alpha particles have a strong charge and travel slowly, they interact significantly with matter that they pass through and may therefore be stopped by a sheet of paper or a few inches of air. Alpha particles cannot penetrate the skin.

Beta Particles

Beta particles are the products of beta decay. Beta particles may be high-speed electrons or high-speed positrons. These two forms of beta decay are designated by the Greek letter beta as β^- and β^+ or ${}^{0}_{-1}e$ and ${}^{0}_{+1}e$, respectively. Negative beta particles are created during radioactive decay when a neutron changes into a proton and an electron. Positive beta particles are created when a proton changes into a neutron and a positron. Beta particles have a greater penetrating ability than alpha particles. Beta particles can be stopped by thin plywood or metal or several feet of air.

Gamma Radiation

Gamma radiation (represented by the Greek letter gamma, γ) is released during gamma decay. Often, atoms that have just undergone alpha or beta decay then undergo gamma decay. An atom produced during alpha or beta decay may still be in an excited state. The atom then releases this energy in a burst of gamma rays as high-energy photons. Gamma radiation is part of the electromagnetic spectrum and consists of electromagnetic waves that travel at the speed of light with frequencies higher than x-rays. Because gamma radiation has no charge, it easily penetrates solid substances. Gamma decay is useful in medical procedures, including cancer treatment.

Radioactive Decay and Half-Life

Radioactivity or radioactive decay occurs when an unstable atom splits to form a more stable atom and emits some type of radiation. An atom's nucleus contains protons and neutrons. The protons have positive charges and repel each other, but the repulsive force between protons is only relevant over very small distances. The neutrons help separate the protons, enabling the strong nuclear force to hold the atom together. As the atomic number increases, this becomes more and more difficult. All atoms with atomic numbers greater than 83 are unstable. The three basic types of radioactive decay are alpha decay, beta decay, and gamma decay. The *half-life* is the length of time it takes for one-half of the atoms of a radioactive substance to decay into a new type of atom.

FISSION REACTION

A typical fission reaction is the fission of uranium-235 from neutron bombardment:

$^{235}_{92}U + ^{1}_{0}n \rightarrow ^{139}_{56}Ba + ^{94}_{36}Kr + 3\ ^{1}_{0}n.$

The uranium-235 atom ($^{235}_{92}U$) is bombarded by a neutron ($^{1}_{0}n$). This neutron is absorbed, forcing the uranium-235 atom into an excited, unstable state. This excited, unstable uranium-235 atom splits into smaller more stable pieces, which consist of a barium-139 atom ($^{139}_{56}Ba$), a krypton-94 atom ($^{94}_{36}Kr$), and three neutrons ($^{1}_{0}n$). These neutrons in turn may bombard other uranium-235 atoms causing the nuclear fission to continue.

NUCLEAR FUSION

Nuclear fusion is the process in which the nuclei of light, unstable atoms unite or fuse to form a heavier, more stable atom. Fusion requires extremely high temperatures and often pressures that force the atoms into a plasma state. In this high-energy state, the atoms collide frequently and are able to fuse together. In this process, some mass is lost and released as large quantities of energy. The Sun's heat and light are produced by a fusion reaction in the Sun's core of four hydrogen atoms fusing into a helium nucleus.

ALPHA EMISSION

In alpha emission, the parent nuclide spits into two parts consisting of the daughter nuclide and an alpha particle. The alpha particle is identical to a helium nucleus and consists of two protons and two neutrons as represented by $^{4}_{2}He$ or $^{4}_{2}He^{2+}$. The daughter nuclide has a mass number that is four less than the parent nuclide and an atomic number that is two less than the parent nuclide. An example of alpha emission is the decay of an uranimum-238 atom into a thorium-234 atom and an alpha particle as shown below:

$$^{238}_{92}U \rightarrow ^{234}_{90}Th + ^{4}_{2}He.$$

POSITIVE AND NEGATIVE BETA DECAY

In positive beta decay, also known as positron emission, the parent nuclide splits into two parts consisting of the daughter nuclide and a positron. The positron is represented by $_{+1}^{0}e$ because its mass is negligible compared to a neutron or proton, and its charge is + 1. The daughter nuclide has the same mass number as the parent nuclide and an atomic number of one less than the parent nuclide. An example of positive beta decay is when a carbon-11 atom splits into a boron-11 atom and a positron as given by the equation shown here:

$$^{11}_{6}C \rightarrow ^{11}_{5}B + _{+1}^{0}e.$$

In negative beta decay, also simply called beta decay, the parent nuclide splits into two parts consisting of the daughter nuclide and an electron. The electron is represented by $_{-1}^{0}e$ because its mass is negligible compared to a neutron or proton, and its charge is −1. An example of negative beta decay is when a carbon-14 atom splits into a nitrogen-14 atom and an electron as given by the following equation:

$$^{14}_{6}C \rightarrow ^{14}_{7}N + _{-1}^{0}e.$$

ELECTRON CAPTURE

In electron capture, an electron from an atom's own electron cloud impacts the atom's nucleus and causes a decay reaction. The parent nuclide absorbs the electron, and a proton is converted to a neutron. A neutrino is emitted from the nucleus. Gamma radiation is also emitted. The daughter nuclide has the same mass number as the parent nuclide, and the atomic number of the daughter nuclide is one lower that the atomic number of the parent nuclide. An example of electron capture is when a nitrogen-13 atom absorbs an electron and converts to a carbon-13 atom while emitting a neutrino ($^{0}_{0}\nu$) and gamma radiation (γ) as shown by the following equation:

$$^{13}_{7}\text{N} + {}^{0}_{-1}\text{e} \rightarrow {}^{13}_{6}\text{C} + {}^{0}_{0}\nu + \gamma.$$

Transmutation

Transmutation is a type of nuclear decay in which an atom is bombarded by high-speed particles to cause it to convert from one type of atom to another type of atom. Ernest Rutherford was the first to accomplish this with the transmutation of the nitrogen-14 atom into an oxygen-17 atom by bombardment with a beam of high-speed helium ions. In this transmutation, the helium-4 ion is also converted to a hydrogen-1 ion:

$$^{14}_{7}\text{N} + {}^{4}_{2}\text{He} \rightarrow {}^{17}_{8}\text{O} + {}^{1}_{1}\text{H}.$$

Neutron Radiation

Neutron radiation is a type of transmutation that is used to create many isotopes that do not occur naturally. In neutron radiation, an atom is bombarded by high-speed neutrons ($^{1}_{0}\text{n}$) to cause nuclear decay. In neutron radiation, the daughter nuclide has a mass number one higher than the parent nuclide but the atomic number remains the same. The daughter is an atom of the same element as the parent nuclide but has one more neutron, which makes it a different isotope of that element. An example of neutron radiation is when a cobalt-59 atom is bombarded by a high-speed neutron and converts to a cobalt-60 atom as shown in the following equation:

$$^{59}_{27}\text{Co} + {}^{1}_{0}\text{n} \rightarrow {}^{60}_{27}\text{Co}.$$

Balancing a Nuclear Reaction

When balancing a nuclear reaction, two key principles must be applied. First, the mass number must be conserved. Second, the atomic number must be conserved. To determine the products formed, the mass numbers and atomic numbers of the particles emitted or absorbed must be known. Alpha decay emits alpha particles ($^{4}_{2}\text{He}$). Beta decay emits electrons ($^{0}_{-1}\text{e}$). Positron decay emits positrons ($^{0}_{+1}\text{e}$). Neutron radiation absorbs neutrons ($^{1}_{0}\text{n}$). In alpha decay, the mass number decreases by four, and the atomic number decreases by two. In negative beta decay, the mass number stays the same and the atomic number increases by one. In positive beta decay, the mass number stays the same and the atomic number decreases by one. In neutron radiation, the mass number increases by one and the atomic number stays the same.

Complete or Balance the Following Nuclear Reactions:

1. $^{230}_{90}\textbf{Th} \leftrightarrow {}^{4}_{2}\textbf{He}$ + ____.

2. $^{40}_{19}\textbf{K} \leftrightarrow {}^{0}_{-1}\textbf{e}$ + ____.

The key principles to completing or balancing nuclear reactions are that the mass number is conserved and the atomic number is conserved.

In number 1, thorium-230 under goes alpha decay and emits an alpha particle with a mass number of 4 and an atomic number of 2. Balancing the atomic numbers (90 – 2) yields an atomic number of

88, which corresponds to radium. Balancing the mass numbers (230 – 4) yields 226. Therefore, the missing product is $^{226}_{88}Ra$.

In number 2, potassium-40 undergoes beta decay and emits an electron with an assigned mass number of 0 and an assigned atomic number of −1. Balancing the atomic numbers (19 – (−1)) yields an atomic number of 20, which corresponds to calcium. Balancing the mass numbers (40 – 0) yields a mass number of 40. Therefore, the missing product is $^{40}_{20}Ca$.

Organic Chemistry

Biochemical Compounds

The four major classes of biochemical compounds are carbohydrates, lipids, proteins, and nucleic acids. Examples of carbohydrates include monosaccharides such as glucose, fructose, and ribose; disaccharides such as sucrose and lactose; and polysaccharides such as starch, cellulose, and glycogen. Examples of lipids include fatty acids, triglycerides, oils, lard, fat-soluble vitamins, waxes, and steroids such as cholesterol. Examples of proteins include enzymes, albumin, keratin, elastin, tubulin, collagen, hemoglobin, histones, and many hormones. Examples of nucleic acids include deoxyribonucleic acid (DNA) and ribonucleic acid (RNA).

Carbohydrates

Carbohydrates are organic compounds that produce energy. The empirical formula for most carbohydrates is CH_2O, which indicates that the ratio of carbon, hydrogen, and oxygen is always 1:2:1.The structure generally consists of aldehydes and ketones containing many hydroxyl groups. In general, carbohydrates are sugars and starches. Carbohydrates can be grouped as simple sugars or complex carbohydrates. The simple sugars include monosaccharides such as glucose and ribose and disaccharides such as sucrose and lactose. Complex carbohydrates are polymers of monosaccharides and include the polysaccharides such as cellulose, starch, and glycogen.

Monosaccharides, Disaccharides, and Polysaccharides

Monosaccharides, disaccharides, and polysaccharides are special types of organic compounds called carbohydrates, which are compounds composed of carbon, hydrogen, and oxygen. Monosaccharides and disaccharides are sugars. Monosaccharides are the simplest carbohydrates. Examples of monosaccharides are glucose, fructose (fruit sugar), ribose, and galactose. Disaccharides consist of two monosaccharides joined together. Examples of disaccharides include sucrose (table sugar), which is a compound of glucose and fructose, and lactose (milk sugar), which is a compound of glucose and galactose. Polysaccharides are polymers of monosaccharides. Examples of polysaccharides include cellulose, starch, and glycogen.

Lipids

Lipids have many functions. The main function of lipids is storing energy. One type of lipid is triglycerides, which include fats and oils. Lipids known as phospholipids also form the cell membranes of all plant and animal cells. Lipids can relay messages among cells in the nervous system and in the immune system. Some lipids are steroids, which serve many functions. For example, cholesterol helps make cell membranes pliable, and some steroids make up hormones such as testosterone and estrogen. Fat-soluble vitamins are also steroids.

Proteins

Proteins are polymers of amino acids. The amino acids are joined together by peptide bonds. The two major groups of proteins are fibrous proteins and globular proteins. Fibrous proteins provide structure in cells, bone tissue, connective tissue and line cartilage, tendons, and epidermal tissue. Examples of fibrous proteins include collage, elastin, and keratin. Globular proteins are huge folded molecules that include enzymes, hemoglobin, and some hormones. Antibodies are globular proteins that help defend the body from antigens. Some proteins such as actin and myosin are involved in muscle contraction. Some proteins act as storage containers for amino acids. Other proteins such as hemoglobin help transport materials throughout the body.

DNA AND RNA

DNA, or deoxyribonucleic acid, is a two-stranded molecule in the shape of a double helix. DNA nucleotides consist of a deoxyribose (sugar), a phosphate, and a base. The bases are guanine, thymine, cytosine, and adenine. Guanine always pairs with cytosine, and thymine always pairs with adenine. If the double helix is compared to a twisted ladder, the legs of the ladder are the sugars and phosphates, and the rungs of the ladder consist of the bases. The bases that make up the rungs of the ladder are bound together with hydrogen bonds.

Deoxyribonucleic acid (DNA) and ribonucleic acid (RNA) are both nucleic acids composed of nucleotides, which have three of their four bases in common: guanine, adenine, and cytosine. The sugar in DNA nucleotides is deoxyribose, whereas the sugar in RNA nucleotides is ribose. DNA contains the base thymine, but RNA replaces thymine with uracil. DNA is double-stranded, and RNA is single-stranded. DNA has the shape of a double helix, whereas RNA is complexly folded. DNA stores the genetic information in the nucleus, while RNA has several forms. For example, *m*RNA, or messenger RNA, is a working copy of DNA, and *t*RNA, or transfer RNA, collects the needed amino acids for the ribosomes during the assembling of proteins.

PHOTOSYNTHESIS

Photosynthesis is the food-making process in green plants. Photosynthesis occurs in the chloroplasts of cells in the presence of light and chlorophyll. The reactants are carbon dioxide and water. The energy from the sunlight is absorbed and stored in the glucose molecules. The net equation for photosynthesis can be represented by the following equations:

- carbon dioxide + water + light $\xrightarrow{\text{chlorophyll}}$ glucose + oxygen
- $6CO_2 + 6H_2O + \text{light} \xrightarrow{\text{chlorophyll}} C_6H_{12}O_6 + 6O_2$.

The products of photosynthesis are glucose and oxygen gas. Glucose is a simple carbohydrate or sugar, which is a six-carbon monosaccharide.

RESPIRATION

Cellular respiration is the process in which energy is released from glucose in the form of adenosine triphosphate (ATP). Cellular respiration is the reverse process of photosynthesis. In cellular respiration, glucose is burned or combined with oxygen as shown in the following equations:

- glucose + oxygen → carbon dioxide + water + ATP
- $C_6H_{12}O_6 + 6O_2 \rightarrow 6CO_2 + 6H_2O$.

The products of cellular respiration are carbon dioxide and water. Energy is released from glucose in the form of ATP.

Oxidation-Reduction

Oxidation, Reduction, Oxidizing Agent, Reducing Agent, Oxidation States

Oxidation can be defined as any process involving a loss of one or more electrons.

Reduction can be defined as any process involving a gain of one or more electrons.

Oxidizing agent can be defined as the reactant in an oxidation-reduction reaction that causes oxidation. The *oxidizing agent* is reduced.

Reducing agent can be defined as the reactant in an oxidation-reduction reaction that causes reduction. The *reducing agent* is oxidized.

Oxidation states, also known as oxidation numbers, represent the charge that an atom has in a molecule or ion.

Oxidation State of an Element in a Molecule or Ion

In order to determine the oxidation state of an element in a molecule or ion, apply these general rules: Hydrogen is usually assigned an oxidation state of +1 except for metal hydrides. Oxygen is usually assigned an oxidation state of −2 except for peroxides. Halogens are usually assigned oxidation states of −1 unless they are combined to a more electronegative element. Alkali metals are always assigned oxidation states of +1. Alkaline earth metals are always assigned oxidation states of +2. Finally, the sum of the oxidation states must equal the charge of the molecule or ion.

Problems

Determine the oxidation states for each element in each of the following:

1. H_2O
2. MgF_2
3. $Ca(NO_3)_2$

1. H_2O

   Oxygen is usually assigned an oxidation state of −2, and hydrogen is usually assigned an oxidation state of +1. Check: 2(+1) + (−2) = 0. Therefore, the oxidation states are as follows: hydrogen +1 and oxygen −2.

2. MgF_2

   Halogens are usually assigned an oxidation state of −1, and alkaline earth metals are always assigned an oxidation state of +2. Check: (+2) + 2(−1) = 0. Therefore, the oxidation states are as follows: magnesium +2 and fluorine −1.

3. $Ca(NO_3)_2$

Oxygen is usually assigned an oxidation number of −2, and alkaline earth metals are always assigned an oxidation state of +2. The oxidation state of nitrogen may be found by balancing the charges of the NO_3^-. Let x represent the charge of the nitrogen atom: $x + 3(-2) = -1$. Solving for x yields $x = +5$. Checking: $(+2) + 2[(+5) + 3(-2)] = 0$. Therefore, the oxidation states are as follows: calcium +2, nitrogen +5, and oxygen −2.

Oxidation-Reduction Reactions

An oxidation-reduction reaction is a reaction in which one of the reactants loses one or more electrons and the other reactant gains one or more reactants. The reactant that loses the electron(s) undergoes oxidation. The reactant that gains the electron(s) undergoes reduction. A common phrase to help remember this is *LEO the lion says GER*, where *LEO* represents *loss of electrons is oxidation* and *GER* represents *gain of electrons is reduction.* Oxidation cannot take place without reduction, and reduction cannot take place without oxidation.

To determine if a reaction is an oxidation-reduction reaction, try to determine if one reactant is oxidized and the other reactant is reduced. First, assign oxidation states to each atom in the reaction. Remember that atoms of elements in their uncombined state are always assigned oxidation states of 0. Alkali metals are assigned +1, and alkaline earth metals are assigned +2. Oxygen is usually assigned −2, hydrogen is usually +1, and halogens are usually assigned −1. Write the half-reactions for each atom in the reactants, and determine if any are oxidized and reduced. If an oxidation reaction and a reduction reaction are present, the reaction is an oxidation-reduction reaction.

Problems

Determine whether each of the following reactions is an oxidation-reduction reaction.

1. $2Mg\ (s) + O_2\ (g) \rightarrow 2\ MgO\ (s)$.

2. $Ca\ (s) + 2HCl\ (aq) \rightarrow CaCl_2\ (aq) + H_2\ (g)$.

1. $2Mg(s) + O_2(g) \rightarrow 2MgO(s)$.

Assign oxidation states to each atom in the reaction. Atoms of an element in its uncombined state are always assigned 0. Therefore, both reactants are assigned 0. Oxygen is usually assigned −2, and magnesium is always assigned +2. Write the half-reactions:

- $Mg \rightarrow Mg^{2+} + 2e^-$ oxidation states of magnesium: $0 \rightarrow +2$.
- $O_2 + 2e^- \rightarrow O^{2-}$ oxidation states of oxygen: $0 \rightarrow -2$.

Magnesium is oxidized. Oxygen is reduced. Therefore, this is an oxidation-reduction reaction:

2. $Ca(s) + 2HCl\ (aq) \rightarrow CaCl_2\ (aq) + H_2\ (g)$.

The reactant Ca (s) and the product H_2 (g) are assigned 0. Halogens such as chlorine are usually assigned −1. Hydrogen is usually assigned +1. Alkaline earth metals such as calcium are always assigned +2. Write the half-reactions:

- $Ca \rightarrow Ca^{2+} + 2e^-$ oxidation states of calcium: $0 \rightarrow +2$.
- $2Cl^- \rightarrow 2Cl^-$ oxidation states of chlorine: $-1 \rightarrow -1$.
- $2H^+ + 2e^- \rightarrow H_2$ oxidation states of hydrogen: $+1 \rightarrow 0$.

Calcium is oxidized. Hydrogen is reduced. Therefore, this is an oxidation-reduction reaction.

Periodic Table

Assigning Atomic Symbols to Elements on the Periodic Table

The atomic symbol for many elements is simply the first letter of the element name. For example, the atomic symbol for hydrogen is H, and the atomic symbol for carbon is C. The atomic symbol of other elements is the first two letters of the element name. For example, the atomic symbol for helium is He, and the atomic symbol for cobalt is Co. The atomic symbols of several elements are derived from Latin. For example, the atomic symbol for copper (Cu) is derived from *cuprum,* and the atomic symbol for iron (Fe) is derived from *ferrum.* The atomic symbol for tungsten (W) is derived from the German word *wolfram*.

Groups and Periods

A group is a vertical column of the periodic table. Elements in the same group have the same number of valence electrons. For the representative elements, the number of valence electrons is equal to the group number. Because of their equal valence electrons, elements in the same groups have similar physical and chemical properties. A period is a horizontal row of the periodic table. Atomic number increases from left to right across a row. The period of an element corresponds to the highest energy level of the electrons in the atoms of that element. The energy level increases from top to bottom down a group.

Atomic Number and Atomic Mass

The elements in the periodic table are arranged in order of increasing atomic number first left to right and then top to bottom across the periodic table. The atomic number represents the number of protons in the atoms of that element. Because of the increasing numbers of protons, the atomic mass typically also increases from left to right across a period and from top to bottom down a row. The atomic mass is a weighted average of all the naturally occurring isotopes of an element.

Arrangement of the Transition Elements

The transition elements belong to one of two categories consisting of the transition metals and the inner transition metals. The transition metals are located in the middle of the periodic table, and the inner transition metals are typically set off as two rows by themselves at the bottom of the periodic table. The transition metals correspond to the "*d* block" for orbital filling, and the inner transition metals correspond to the "*f* block" for orbital filling. Examples of transition metals include iron, copper, nickel, and zinc. The inner transition metals consist of the *lanthanide* or *rare-earth series,* which corresponds to the first row, and the *actinide series,* which corresponds to the second row of the inner transition metals. The *lanthanide series* includes lanthanum, cerium, and praseodymium. The *actinide series* includes actinium, uranium, and plutonium.

ARRANGEMENT OF METALS, NONMETALS, AND METALLOIDS

The metals are located on the left side and center of the periodic table, and the nonmetals are located on the right side of the periodic table. The metalloids or semimetals form a zigzag line between the metals and nonmetals as shown below. Metals include the alkali metals such as lithium, sodium, and potassium and the alkaline earth metals such as beryllium, magnesium, and calcium. Metals also include the transition metals such as iron, copper, and nickel and the inner transition metals such as thorium, uranium, and plutonium. Nonmetals include the chalcogens such as oxygen and sulfur, the halogens such as fluorine and chlorine, and the noble gases such as helium and argon. Carbon, nitrogen, and phosphorus are also nonmetals. Metalloids or semimetals include boron, silicon, germanium, antimony, and polonium.

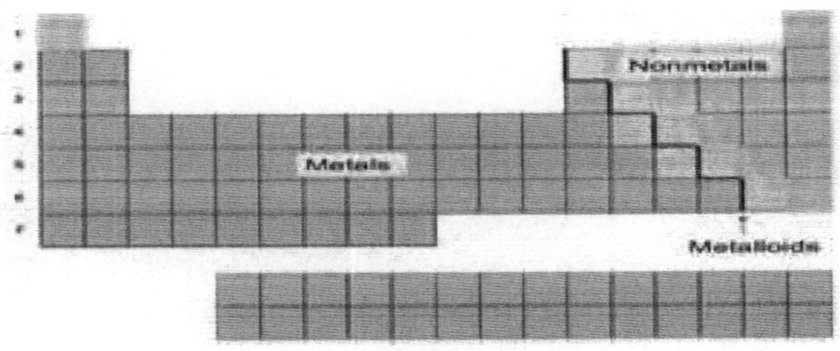

ATOMIC RADIUS SIZE

Atomic radius size decreases across a period from left to right and increases down a group from top to bottom. The atomic radius decreases across a period due to the increasing number of protons and the attraction between those protons and the orbiting electrons. The atomic radius increases down a group due to the increasing energy levels. Atoms in the top-right corner of the periodic table (including hydrogen) have the smallest atomic radii, and atoms in the bottom-left corner of the periodic table have the largest atomic radii. Helium has the smallest atomic radius, and francium has the largest atomic radius.

IONIC RADIUS SIZE

The ionic radius size increases down a group of the periodic table. This is due to the increasing energy levels and the fact that electrons are orbiting farther and farther from the nucleus. The trend seen across the periods of the periodic table is due to the formation of cations or anions. Metals form cations or positive ions. Cations are smaller than their neutral atoms due to the loss of one or more electrons. Nonmetals except the noble gases form anions or negative ions. Anions are larger than their neutral atoms due to the gain of one or more electrons.

IONIZATION ENERGY

Ionization energy is the amount of energy needed to remove an electron from an isolated atom. Ionization energy decreases down a group of the periodic table because the electrons get farther and farther from the nucleus making it easier for the electron to be removed. Ionization energy increases across a period of the periodic table due to the decreasing atomic size, which is due to the increasing number of protons attracting the electrons towards the nucleus. These trends of ionization energy are the opposite of the trends for atomic radius.

ELECTRON AFFINITY

Electron affinity is the energy required to add an electron to a neutral atom in the gaseous phase of an element. Electron affinity values typically range from less negative to more negative. If electrons are added to a halogen such as fluorine or chlorine, energy is released and the electron affinity is negative. If electrons are added to an alkaline earth metal, energy is absorbed and the electron affinity is positive. In general, electron affinity becomes more negative from left to right across a period in the periodic table. Electron affinity becomes less negative from the top to the bottom of a group of the periodic table.

Electronegativity

Electronegativity is a measure of the ability of an atom that is chemically combined to at least one other atom in a molecule to attract electrons to it. The Pauling scale is commonly used to assign values to the elements, with fluorine, which is the most electronegative element, being assigned a value of 4.0. Electronegativity increases from left to right across a period of the periodic table and decreases from top to bottom down a group of the periodic table.

Physical Properties of the Elements

The boiling point, melting point, and conductivity of the elements depend partially on the number of valence electrons of the atoms of those elements. For the representative elements in groups 1A–8A, the number of valence electrons matches the group number. Because all of the elements in each individual group contain the same number of valence electrons, elements in the same groups tend to have similar boiling points, melting points, and conductivity. Boiling points and melting points tend to decrease moving down the column of groups 1A–4A and 8A but increase slightly moving down the column of groups 5A–7A.

Chemical Reactivity of the Elements

Atoms of elements in the same group or family of the periodic table tend to have similar chemical properties and similar chemical reactions. For example, the alkali metals, which form cations with a charge of 1+, tend to react with water to form hydrogen gas and metal hydroxides. The alkaline earth metals, which form cations with a charge of 2+, react with oxygen gas to form metal oxides. The halogens, which form anions with a charge of 1–, are highly reactive and toxic. The noble gases are unreactive and never form compounds naturally.

Physical Behavior of Matter

Pure Substances

Pure substances are substances that cannot be further broken down into simpler substances and still retain their characteristics. Pure substances are categorized as either elements or compounds. Elements that consist of only one type of atom may be monatomic, diatomic, or polyatomic. For example, helium (He) and copper (Cu) are monatomic elements, and hydrogen (H_2) and oxygen (O_2) are diatomic elements. Phosphorus (P_4) and sulfur (S_8) are polyatomic elements. Compounds consist of molecules of more than one type of atom. For example, pure water (H_2O) is made up of molecules consisting of two atoms of hydrogen bonded to one atom of oxygen, and glucose ($C_6H_{12}O_6$) is made up of molecules of six carbon atoms and twelve hydrogen atoms bonded together with six oxygen atoms.

Mixtures

Mixtures can be classified as either homogeneous mixtures or heterogeneous mixtures. The molecules of homogeneous mixtures are distributed uniformly throughout the mixture, but the molecules of heterogeneous mixtures are not distributed uniformly throughout the mixture. Air is an example of a homogeneous mixture, and a pile of sand and salt is an example of a heterogeneous mixture. Solutions are homogeneous mixtures consisting of a solute, the substance that is dissolved, and a solvent, the substance doing the dissolving. Examples of solutions include vinegar (a solution of acetic acid in water) and sugar dissolved in water. Suspensions are heterogeneous mixtures in which the particle size of the substance suspended is too large to be kept in suspension by Brownian motion. Once left undisturbed, suspensions will settle out to form layers. An example of a suspension is sand stirred into water. Left undisturbed, the sand will fall out of suspension and the water will form a layer on top of the sand.

States of Matter

The four states of matter are solids, liquids, gases, and plasma. Solids have a definite shape and a definite volume. Because solid particles are held in fairly rigid positions, solids are the least compressible of the four states of matter. Liquids have definite volumes but no definite shapes. Because their particles are free to slip and slide over each other, liquids take the shape of their containers, but they still remain fairly incompressible by natural means. Gases have no definite shape or volume. Because gas particles are free to move, they move away from each other causing gases to fill their containers. This also makes gases very compressible. Plasmas are high-temperature, ionized gases that exist only under very high temperatures at which electrons are stripped away from their atoms.

Atoms and Ions

Neutral atoms have equal numbers of protons and electrons. Some atoms tend to lose electrons in order to have a full outer shell of valence electrons and become positively charged ions or cations. For example, the alkali metals sodium and potassium form the cations Na^+ and K^+, and the alkaline earth metals magnesium and calcium form the cations Mg^{2+} and Ca^{2+}. Some atoms tend to gain electrons to fill their outer shells and become negatively charged ions or anions. For example, the halogens fluorine and chlorine form the anions F^- and Cl^-, and the chalcogens oxygen and sulfur form the anions O^{2-} and S^{2-}

ATOMS AND MOLECULES

Atoms are the smallest particles of an element that still retain the properties of that element. For example, a copper atom is the smallest piece of a copper wire that still has the properties of copper. Molecules are made of two or more atoms. Molecules are the smallest particles of a compound that still retain the properties of that compound. For example, the substance water consists of water molecules of two hydrogen atoms covalently bonded to one oxygen atom. A water molecule is the smallest particle of water that still has the properties of water. Also, elements may be diatomic or polyatomic molecules. For example, hydrogen gas (H_2) exists naturally as diatomic molecules. In this case, the molecule could be further broken down into individual hydrogen atoms.

KINETIC AND POTENTIAL ENERGY

The internal energy of a system may be categorized as kinetic energy or potential energy. Kinetic energy is the energy of a system associated with movement. In chemical systems, this movement is predicted by the kinetic theory of matter and is due to the random movement of the particles that make up the system. The kinetic energy of a particle may be calculated by the following formula: $KE = \frac{1}{2}mv^2$, where *KE* is the kinetic energy in joules, *m* is the mass of the particle in kilograms, and *v* is the velocity of the particle in meters per second. Potential energy is the stored energy in a system associated with position or configuration. In chemical systems, this energy is the energy associated with the chemical bonds and intermolecular forces of the matter contained in the system.

CHEMICAL, ELECTRICAL, ELECTROMAGNETIC, NUCLEAR, AND THERMAL ENERGY

Different types of energy may be associated with systems. Chemical energy is the energy that is stored in chemical bonds and intermolecular forces. Electrical energy is the energy associated with the movement of electrons or ions through a material. Electromagnetic energy is the energy of electromagnetic waves of several frequencies including radio waves, microwaves, infrared light, visible light, ultraviolet light, x-rays, and gamma rays. Nuclear energy is the binding energy that is stored within an atom's nucleus. Thermal energy is the total internal kinetic energy of a system due to the random motions of the particles.

CONVERSION OF ENERGY WITHIN CHEMICAL SYSTEMS

Chemical energy is the energy stored in molecules in the bonds between the atoms of those molecules and energy associated with the intermolecular forces. This stored potential energy may be converted into kinetic energy and then into heat. During a chemical reaction, atoms may be rearranged and chemical bonds may be formed or broken accompanied by a corresponding absorption or release of energy, usually in the form of heat. According to the first law of thermodynamics, during these energy conversions, the total amount of energy must be conserved.

TEMPERATURE

Temperature is a measure of the average kinetic energy of the atoms or molecules in a system. The Celsius scale is the most commonly used scale with the freezing point of water at 0 °C and the boiling point of water at 100 °C. Normal body temperature is 37 °C. On the Fahrenheit scale, water freezes at 32 °F and boils at 212 °F. Normal body temperature is 98.6 °F. In chemistry, the Kelvin scale is frequently used. Water freezes at 273.15 K and boils at 373.15 K. The Celsius scale and the Kelvin scale have exactly 100 ° between the freezing point and boiling point of water. The Fahrenheit scale has 180 ° between the freezing point and the boiling point of water. The value of 1 °F is 100/180 or 5/9 of the size of 1 °C. The formulas to convert between the temperature scales are as follows: $T_C = \frac{5}{9}(T_F - 32)$; $T_F = \frac{9}{5}T_C + 32$; $T_K = T_C + 273.15$.

PROBLEMS

PERFORM THE FOLLOWING TEMPERATURE CONVERSIONS.

1. Convert 200.0 °F to the Celsius scale.
2. Convert 24.0 °C to the Fahrenheit scale.
3. Convert 21.5 °C to the Kelvin scale.

1. To convert from 200.0 °F to °C, use the equation $T_C = \frac{5}{9}(T_F - 32)$. Substituting 200.0 in for T_F yields $T_C = \frac{5}{9}(200.0 - 32) = \frac{5}{9}(168.0) = 93.33$ °C.

2. To convert from 24.0 °C to °F, use the equation $T_F = \frac{9}{5}T_C + 32$. Substituting 24.0 in for T_C yields T_F =

$$\frac{9}{5}(24.0) + 32 = 43.2 + 32 = 75.2 \text{ °F}.$$

3. To convert from 21.5 °C to K, use the equation $T_K = T_C + 273.15$. Substituting 21.5 in for T_C yields $T_K = 21.5 + 273.15 = 294.7$ K.

THERMAL ENERGY

Thermal energy is part of a system's total internal energy, which consists of potential and kinetic energy. Thermal energy is the total internal kinetic energy of a system due to the random motions of the particles. The thermal energy of a system is measured by its temperature, which is the average kinetic energy of the particles in that system. The flow of thermal energy is referred to as heat. Appropriate units for thermal energy include the joule (J), British thermal unit (Btu) (1 Btu = 1,055 J), calorie (1 calorie = 4.1868 J), and Calorie (1 Calorie = 1 kilocalorie).

HEAT TRANSFER

Heat transfer is the flow of thermal energy, which is measured by temperature. Heat will flow from warmer objects to cooler objects until an equilibrium is reached in which both objects are at the same temperature. Because the particles of warmer objects possess a higher kinetic energy than the particles of cooler objects, the particles of the warmer objects are vibrating more quickly and collide more often, transferring energy to the cooler objects in which the particles have less kinetic energy and are moving more slowly. Heat may be transferred by conduction, convection, or radiation. In conduction, heat is transferred by direct contact between two objects. In convection, heat is transferred by moving currents. In radiation, heat is transferred by electromagnetic waves.

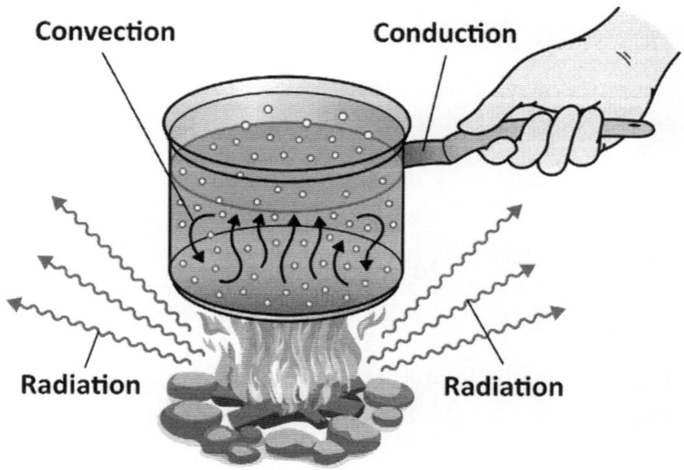

EXAMPLE

Calculate the amount of heat lost by a piece of copper with a mass of 100.0 g when it cools from 100.0 °C to 20.0 °C. The specific heat of copper is 0.380 J/(g·°C).

To calculate the amount of heat lost by a piece of copper with a mass of 100.0 g when it cools from 100.0 °C to 20.0 °C, use the equation $Q = mc\Delta T$, where Q is the amount of heat lost in joules, m is the mass of the copper in grams, c is the specific heat of copper, and ΔT is the change in temperature $T_2 - T_1$ in degrees Celsius. Substituting 100.0 g for m, 0.380 J/(g·°C) for c, 20.0 °C for T_2, and 100.0 °C for T_1 yields Q = (100.0 g)(0.380 J/(g·°C))(20.0 °C – 100.0 °C) = –3,040 J. The negative value confirms that heat was lost as the copper cooled.

HEAT CAPACITY AND SPECIFIC HEAT

Heat capacity is the amount of heat required to raise a sample of matter by 1 °C. Heat capacity is an extensive property and varies with the amount of matter in the sample. The greater the mass of the sample, the higher the heat capacity of the sample. This means that a specific type of matter will have different heat capacities depending on the size of the sample. Heat capacity may be represented by the formula $C = \frac{Q}{\Delta T}$, where Q is the heat in joules and ΔT is the change in temperature in degrees Celsius. Specific heat is the amount of heat required to raise the temperature of a unit mass by 1 °. The formula for specific heat is $c = \frac{Q}{m\Delta T}$, where Q is the heat in joules, ΔT is the change in temperature in degrees Celsius, and m is the mass of the sample. Because the specific heat formula incorporates the mass of the sample, a specific type of substance will have a constant specific heat, making specific heat an intensive property.

CALORIMETER

The specific heat of a substance can be determined using a calorimeter. A known amount of the substance is heated to a known temperature. In the classroom setting, this can be accomplished by placing the metal in a loosely stoppered test tube and then placing the test tube in boiling water. The calorimeter is prepared by placing water of a known amount and temperature in the calorimeter. The heated metal is carefully placed into the water in the calorimeter. The temperature of the water is carefully monitored until it stops rising. The final temperature of the metal will be equal to the final temperature of the water. The heat lost by the metal equals the heat gained by the water as shown by the following equations:

$Q_{\text{lost by the metal}} = Q_{\text{gained by the water}}$

$-m_{\text{metal}}\, c_{\text{metal}}\, \Delta T_{\text{metal}} = m_{\text{water}}\, c_{\text{water}}\, \Delta T_{\text{water}}$, where Q is the amount of heat lost or gained in joules, m is the mass in grams, c is the specific heat, and ΔT is the change in temperature $T_2 - T_1$ in degrees Celsius.

Calorimetry Problem

In a calorimetry experiment, to determine the specific heat of an unknown metal with a mass of 100.0 g, the temperature of the unknown metal dropped 20.0° C. The temperature of the water with a mass of 100.0 g in the calorimeter raised 1.00 °C.

Explain how to find the specific heat of the unknown metal. Use 4.20 J/(g·°C) for the specific heat of water.

The heat lost by the metal must equal the heat gained by the water as shown in the equation

$Q_{\text{lost by metal}} = Q_{\text{gained by the water}}$, where Q is the amount of heat lost or gained in joules. To calculate the specific heat of the metal, use the equation $-m_{\text{metal}}\, c_{\text{metal}}\, \Delta T_{\text{metal}} = m_{\text{water}}\, c_{\text{water}}\, \Delta T_{\text{water}}$, where m is the mass of the metal or water in grams, c is the specific heat of the metal or water, and ΔT is the change in temperature $(T_2 - T_1)$ in degrees Celsius in the metal or water. Solving the equation for c_{metal} results in $c_{\text{metal}} = -\frac{m_{\text{water}}\, c_{\text{water}}\, \Delta T_{\text{water}}}{m_{\text{metal}} \Delta T_{\text{metal}}}$. Substituting in the given information yields $c_{\text{metal}} = -\frac{(100.0\text{ g})(4.20\text{ J/g·°C})(1.00\text{ °C})}{(100.0\text{ g})(20.0\text{ °C})} = 0.21\text{ J/g·°C}$.

Heat of Vaporization, Heat of Fusion, and Heat of Sublimation

The *heat of vaporization* (ΔH_{vap}) is the amount of heat that must be added to one mole of a substance to change the substance from the liquid phase to the gaseous phase.

The *heat of fusion* (ΔH_{fus}) is the amount of heat that must be added to one mole of a substance to change the substance from the solid phase to the liquid phase.

The *heat of sublimation* (ΔH_{sub}) is the amount of heat that must be added to one mole of a substance to change the substance directly from the solid phase to the gaseous phase without passing through the liquid phase.

Phase Diagram

A phase diagram is a graph or chart of pressure versus temperature that represents the solid, liquid, and gaseous phases of a substance and the transitions between these phases. Typically, pressure is located on the vertical axis, and temperature is located along the horizontal axis. The curves drawn on the graph represent points at which different phases are in an equilibrium state. These curves indicate at which pressure and temperature the phase changes of sublimation, melting, and boiling occur. Specifically, the curve between the liquid and gas phases indicates the pressures and temperatures at which the liquid and gas phases are in equilibrium. The curve between the solid and liquid phases indicates the temperatures and pressures at which the solid and liquid phases are in equilibrium. The open spaces on the graph represent the distinct phases solid, liquid, and gas. The point at which the solid–liquid, solid–gas, and liquid–gas phase boundaries intersect is called the triple point. At the triple point, the solid, liquid, and gas phases all exist in equilibrium. The critical point, by contrast, is the endpoint of the liquid–gas coexistence curve, where the liquid and gas phases become indistinguishable and form a supercritical fluid.

EXPLANATION OF THE LETTERED REGIONS OF A PHASE DIAGRAM

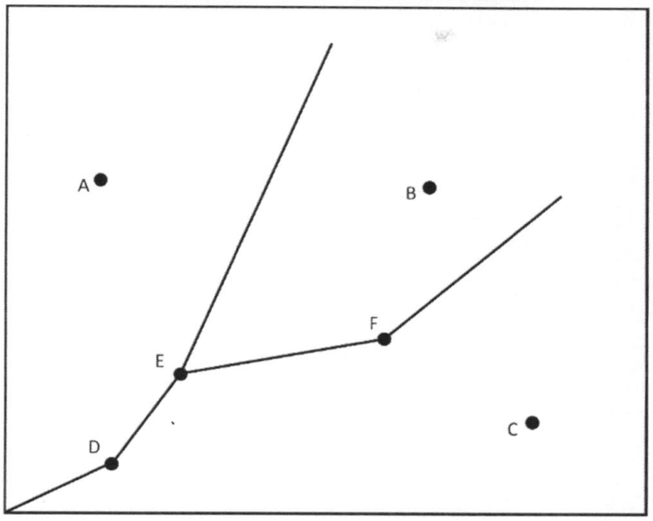

A—Solid phase: This is a region of high pressure and low temperature where the substance always exists as a solid.

B—Liquid phase: This is a region of pressure and temperature where the substance is in the liquid phase

C—Gas phase: This is a region of pressure and temperature where the substance is in the gaseous phase.

D—Sublimation point: The portion of the curve that contains point D shows all the combinations of pressure and temperature at which the solid phase is in equilibrium with the gaseous phase.

E—Triple point: The point at which the solid, liquid, and gaseous phases are all in equilibrium.

F—Boiling point: The line that contains point F indicates all the combinations of pressure and temperature at which the liquid phase and gas phase are in equilibrium.

PROBLEM #1

Calculate the amount of heat required to change 100.0 g of ice at –10.0 °C to water at 10.0 °C. (ΔH_{fus} = 334 J/g; c_{water} = 4.18 J/(g·°C), c_{ice} = 2.06 J/(g·°C)).

To calculate the amount of heat required to change 100.0 g of ice at –10.0 °C to water at 10.0 °C, it is necessary to calculate the heat required each step along the way. Step 1 is to calculate the heat required to raise the temperature of the ice from –10.0 °C to 0.0 °C. Step 2 is to calculate the amount of heat required to melt the ice. Finally, step 3 is to calculate the amount of heat required to raise the temperature of the water from 0.0 °C to 10.0 °C. For steps 1 and 3, the required equation is $Q = mc\Delta T$. Because step 2 is a phase change, the required equation is $Q = m\Delta H_{fus}$. For step 1: Q_1 = (100.0 g)(2.06 J/(g·°C))(0.0 °C – (–10.0 °C)) = 2,060 J. For step 2: Q_2 =

$m\Delta H_{fus}$ = (100.0 g)(334 J/g) = 33,400 J. For step 3: Q_1 = (100.0 g)(4.18 J/(g·°C))(10.0 °C – 0.0 °C) = 4,180 J. Adding $Q_1 + Q_2 + Q_3$ = 2,060 J + 33,400 J + 4,180 J = 39,640 J.

PROBLEM #2

Calculate the amount of heat required to change 100.0 g of water at 90.0 °C to steam at 110.0 °C (ΔH_{vap} = 2,260 J/g; c_{steam} = 1.86 J/(g·°C), c_{water} = 4.18 J/(g·°C)).

To calculate the amount of heat required to change 100.0 g of water at 90.0 °C to steam at 110.0 °C, it is necessary to calculate the heat required at each step along the way. Step 1 is to calculate the heat required to raise the temperature of the water from 90.0 °C to 100.0 °C. Step 2 is to calculate the amount of heat required to change the water to steam. Finally, step 3 is to calculate the amount of heat required to raise the temperature of the steam from 100.0 °C to 110.0 °C. For steps 1 and 3, the required equation is $Q = mc\Delta T$. Because Step 2 is a phase change, the required equation is $Q = m\Delta H_{vap}$. For step 1: Q_1 = (100.0 g)(4.18 J/(g·°C))(100.0 °C – 90.0 °C) = 4,180 J. For step 2: $Q_2 = m\Delta H_{vap}$ = (100.0 g)(2,260 J/g) = 226,000 J. For step 3: Q_1 = (100.0 g)(1.86 J/(g·°C))(110.0 °C – 100.0 °C) = 1,860 J. Adding Q1 + Q2 + Q3 = 4,180 J + 226,000 J + 1,860 J = 232,040 J.

HEATING CURVE OF WATER

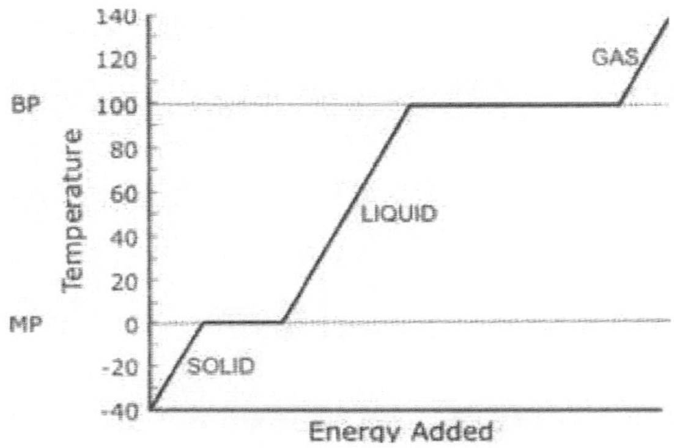

In the first portion of the curve, the graph slants up and to the right as the ice is a solid that is increasing in temperature from −10 °C to 0 °C. In the second portion of the curve, the graph remains horizontal during the phase change from solid to liquid as the temperature remains constant at 0 °C. In the third portion of the curve, the graph slants up and to the right as the water now is in the liquid state and is increasing in temperature from 0 °C to 100 °C. In the fourth portion of the curve, the graph remains horizontal during the phase change from liquid to gas as the temperature remains at 100 °C. In the last portion of the curve, the graph slants up and to the right as water now is the gaseous state and the steam is increasing in temperature from 100 °C to 110 °C.

CALCULATING THE AMOUNT OF HEAT REQUIRED DURING EACH PORTION OF THE HEATING CURVE

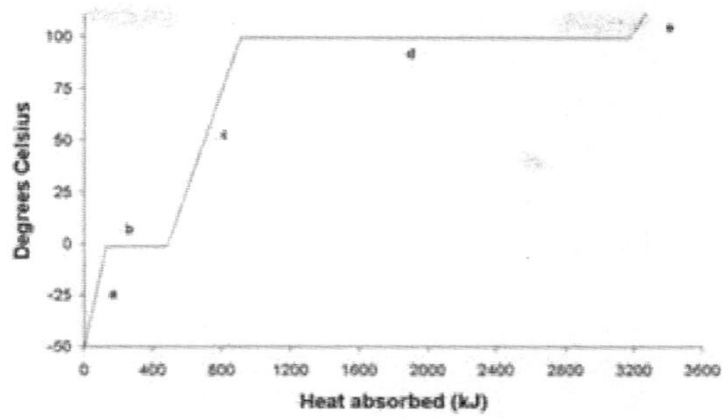

For portion a, $Q = mc_{ice}\Delta T$, where Q is the amount of heat gained in joules, m is the mass of the ice in grams, c is the specific heat of ice, and ΔT is the change in temperature in degrees Celsius.

For portion b, $Q = m\Delta H_{fus}$, where Q is the amount of heat gained in joules, m is the mass of the ice/water in grams, and ΔH_{fus} is the heat of fusion for water in joules/gram.

For portion c, $Q = mc_{water}\Delta T$, where Q is the amount of heat gained in joules, m is the mass of the water in grams, c is the specific heat of water, and ΔT is the change in temperature in degrees Celsius.

For portion d, $Q = m\Delta H_{vap}$, where Q is the amount of heat gained in joules, m is the mass of the water/steam in grams, and ΔH_{vap} is the heat of fusion for water in joules/gram.

For portion e, $Q = mc_{steam}\Delta T$, where Q is the amount of heat gained in joules, m is the mass of the steam in grams, c is the specific heat of steam, and ΔT is the change temperature in degrees Celsius.

ASSUMPTIONS OF THE KINETIC MOLECULAR THEORY

The kinetic molecular theory consists of several assumptions including the following:

- Ideal gas molecules are in constant random motion. The gas molecules travel in straight lines until they collide with other gas molecules or with the walls of the container.
- Ideal gas molecules have a negligible volume compared to the volume of the gas itself. Most of the volume of a gas is empty space.
- Ideal gas molecules exert no attractive or repulsive forces on each other.
- Ideal gas molecules have a kinetic energy that is directly proportional to the absolute temperature. The higher the temperature, the higher the average kinetic energy of the gas molecules, and the faster the gas molecules are moving.
- Ideal gas molecules have perfectly elastic collisions. The kinetic energy lost by one gas molecule is gained by another gas molecule. No energy is lost in the collision with the container.

IDEAL GASES, AND SHORTCOMINGS OF ASSUMING AN IDEAL GAS

An ideal gas is a hypothetical or theoretical gas. Ideal gases are assumed to be a set of randomly moving point particles that do not interact with each other. The collisions of ideal gases are assumed to be completely elastic, and the intermolecular forces are assumed to be zero. Real gases show more complex behaviors. The ideal gas laws tend to fail at low temperatures and high pressures when the effects of the particle size and intermolecular forces are more apparent. Also, the idea gas assumptions do not account for phase transitions.

Boyle's Law

Boyle's law describes the relationship between the volume and pressure of an ideal gas at a constant temperature for a given amount of gas. For an ideal gas, volume and pressure are inversely related. Because gases are compressible, if the pressure of a gas sample is increased, the volume will decrease. If the pressure of a gas sample is decreased, the volume will increase. Conversely, if the volume of a gas sample is increased, the pressure will decrease. If the volume of a gas sample is decreased, the pressure will increase. For example, if the pressure of a gas sample is doubled, the volume decreases to one-half of the original volume. If the pressure of a gas sample is tripled, the volume decreases to one-third of the original volume. The relationship between volume and pressure is represented by $V \propto \frac{1}{P}$ or $V = k\frac{1}{P}$ or $PV = k$. Because the product of the pressure and the volume is a constant, Boyle's law can be stated as $P_iV_i = P_fV_f$.

Charles's Law

Charles's law describes the relationship between the volume and temperature of an ideal gas at a constant pressure for a given amount of gas. For an ideal gas, volume and temperature are directly related. Because the kinetic energy of a gas is directly proportional to the absolute temperature, if the temperature increases, the average kinetic energy of the gas molecules increases. As the molecules move faster, they spread farther apart, increasing the volume. If the volume of the container is increased, the temperature will also increase due to the fact the molecules will have to move faster to strike the container more often because the pressure must remain constant. The relationship between volume and pressure is represented by $V \propto T$ or $V = kT$ or $\frac{V}{T} = k$. Because the quotient of the volume and the temperature is a constant, Charles's law can be stated as $\frac{V_i}{T_i} = \frac{V_f}{T_f}$, where the temperature is stated in kelvin.

Avogadro's Law

Avogadro's law describes the relationship between the volume and amount in moles of an ideal gas at a constant pressure and temperature. For an ideal gas, the volume and the number of moles are directly related. If the volume increases, the number of moles would have to increase in order to maintain the pressure and temperature. If the number of moles in the container increases, the volume will also need to increase to maintain the same pressure and temperature. The relationship between volume and amount in mole of a gas is represented by $V \propto N, V = kN$, or $\frac{V}{N} = k$. Because the quotient of the volume and the amount in moles is a constant, Avogadro's law can be stated as $\frac{V_i}{N_i} = \frac{V_f}{N_f}$.

Combined Gas Law

The combined gas law combines Boyle's law and Charles's law. According to Boyle's law, volume and pressure are inversely related, or $V \propto \frac{1}{P}$. According to Charles's law, volume and temperature are directly related, or $V \propto T$. Combining these relationships into one yields $V \propto \frac{T}{P}$ or $V = k\frac{T}{P}$.

Solving for k yields $\frac{PV}{T}$. Because $k = \frac{P_1V_1}{T_1}$ and $k = \frac{P_2V_2}{T_2}$, the combined gas law can be written as $\frac{P_1V_1}{T_1} = \frac{P_2V_2}{T_2}$. For situations in which $V_1 = V_2$, the combined gas law yields a relationship of $P \propto T$, indicating that for a constant volume, the pressure and temperature are directly related.

Ideal Gas Law

The ideal gas law combines Boyle's law, Charles's law, and Avogadro's law. According to Boyle's law, $V \propto \frac{1}{P}$. According to Charles's law, $V \propto T$. According to Avogadro's law, $V \propto n$. Combining these three relationships into one relationship yields $V \propto \frac{nT}{P}$. Multiplying through by P yields $PV \propto nT$, or $PV = nRT$, where R is the ideal gas constant of 0.0821 L·atm/(K·mol), P is the pressure in atm, V is the volume in L, n is the number of moles in mol, and T is the temperature in K.

Behavior of Real Gases

Although assuming that gases are ideal is appropriate for many situations, real gases behave differently than ideal gases. The collisions of real gases are not elastic. Real gases do have attractive and repulsive forces. Real gases have mass, whereas ideal gases do not. The atoms or molecules of real gases are not point particles, and they do interact with each other especially under high pressures and low temperatures. Under the right conditions of pressure and temperature, real gases will undergo phase transitions and become liquids. The pressure of real gases is less than those of ideal gases due to the small attractive forces between the particles in the gases.

Problem #1

A 5.0 L gas sample has a pressure of 1.0 standard atmosphere (atm). If the pressure is increased to 2.0 atm, find the new volume. Assume that the temperature is constant.

To find the new volume, use the equation associated with Boyle's law $P_iV_i = P_fV_f$. Solving the equation for the unknown V_f yields $V_f = \frac{P_iV_i}{P_f}$. Substituting in the given values $P_i = 1.0$ atm, $V_i = 5.0$ L, and $P_f = 2.0$ atm into the equation yields $V_f = \frac{(1.0\text{ atm})(5.0\text{ L})}{(2.0\text{ atm})} = 2.5$ L. This checks because the pressure increased and the volume decreased. More specifically, because the pressure was doubled, the volume was reduced to one-half of the original volume.

Problem #2

A gas sample has a volume of 10.0 L at 200.0 K. Find its volume if the temperature is increased to 300.0 K.

To find the new volume, use the equation associated with Charles's law $\frac{V_i}{T_i} = \frac{V_f}{T_f}$.

Solving the equation for the unknown V_f yields $V_f = \frac{T_fV_i}{T_i}$. Substituting the given values $V_i = 10.0$ L, $T_i = 200.0$ K, and $T_f = 300.0$ K into the equation yields $V_f = \frac{(300.0\text{ K})(10.0\text{ L})}{(200.0\text{ K})} = 15.0$ L. This checks because the temperature increased and the volume increased. Also, note that if the temperature had not been stated in kelvin, it would have to be converted to kelvin before substituting the values in to the equation.

Problem #3

Find the pressure that 0.500 mol of H_2 (g) will exert on a 500.0 mL flask at 300.0 K.

To calculate the pressure that 0.500 mol of H_2 will exert on a 500.0 mL flask at 300.0 K, use the ideal gas equation $PV = nRT$, where R is the ideal gas constant of 0.0821 L·atm/(K·mol), P is the pressure in atm, V is the volume in L, n is the number of moles in mol, and T is the temperature in kelvin. Solving the ideal gas equation for P yields $P = \frac{nRT}{V}$. First, convert the 500.0 mL to 0.500 L. Substituting in n = 0.500 mol, V = 0.500 L, T = 300.0 K, and $R = 0.0821 \frac{\text{L·atm}}{\text{K·mol}}$ yields $P = \frac{(0.500\text{ mol})(0.0821\text{ L·atm/(K·mol)})(300.0\text{ K})}{(0.500\text{ L})} = 24.6\text{ atm}$.

Behavior of Real Gases

Although assuming that gases are ideal is appropriate for many situations, real gases behave differently than ideal gases. The collisions of real gases are not elastic. Real gases do have attractive and repulsive forces. Real gases have mass, whereas ideal gases do not. The atoms or molecules of real gases are not point particles, and they do interact with each other especially under high pressures and low temperatures. Under the right conditions of pressure and temperature, real gases will undergo phase transitions and become liquids. The pressure of real gases is less than those of ideal gases due to the small attractive forces between the particles in the gases.

Exothermic and Endothermic Reactions

Exothermic reactions release heat energy, whereas endothermic reactions absorb energy. Exothermic reactions can be represented by reactants → products + heat. Endothermic reactions can be represented by reactants + heat → products. The change in enthalpy for exothermic reactions is negative, whereas the change in enthalpy for endothermic reactions is positive. An example of an exothermic reaction is the burning of propane. An example of an endothermic reaction is the reaction that takes place in a first-aid cold pack.

Hess's Law

Bond energy is the energy needed to break or form a bond. Hess's law can be used to calculate bond energy. Usually, Hess's law is used to state the relationship between the enthalpies of formations of the reactants and the enthalpies of formation of the products of a reaction. Basically, Hess's law states that when reactants are converted to products, the total sum of the energy required to break the bonds of the reactants minus the total sum of energy required to form the bonds of the products is equal to the heat of the reaction. Enthalpies of formation are generally used in place of the actual bond energies because enthalpies of formation have been standardized whereas the bond energies of individual molecules vary. Hess's law is given by the equation $\Delta H^\circ_{\text{reaction}} = \Sigma \Delta H^\circ_{f(\text{products})} - \Sigma \Delta H^\circ_{f(\text{reactants})}$.

PROBLEM

Calculate the $\Delta H°$ for the following reaction: $3\ H_2(g) + N_2(g) \rightarrow 2\ NH_3(g)$ (ammonia: $\Delta H_f° = -46.19$ kJ/mol).

To calculate the $\Delta H°$ for the following reaction: $3\ H_2(g) + N_2(g) \rightarrow 2\ NH_3(g)$ given that for ammonia $\Delta H_f° = -46.19$ kJ/mol, use the equation given by Hess's law: $\Delta H^{\circ}_{\text{reaction}} = \Sigma \Delta H^{\circ}_{f(\text{products})} - \Sigma \Delta H^{\circ}_{f(\text{reactants})}$. Recall that the enthalpy of formation (ΔH°_f) of an element in its uncombined state is zero. The number of moles of each reactant and product is the coefficients from the balanced chemical equation. Substituting this information and the given information into the equation yields $\Delta H^{\circ}_{\text{reaction}} = \Sigma \Delta H^{\circ}_{f(\text{products})} - \Sigma \Delta H^{\circ}_{f(\text{reactants})} = [(2\text{ mol})(-46.19\text{ kJ/mol})] - [(3\text{ mol})(0\text{ kJ/mol}) + (1\text{ mol})(0\text{ kJ/mol})] = -92.38\text{ kJ}$.

PROBLEMS

EXPLAIN WHICH INTERMOLECULAR INTERACTIONS ARE PRESENT IN EACH OF THE FOLLOWING:

1. NH_3
2. CH_4
3. H_2S

1. NH_3

The intermolecular forces present in a sample of NH_3 are London forces and hydrogen bonds. London forces are present between all molecules. Hydrogen bonds are present between molecules with hydrogen covalently bonded to nitrogen, fluorine, and oxygen.

2. CH_4

The intermolecular forces present in a sample of CH_4 are only London forces. London forces are present between all molecules. Because CH_4 is a nonpolar molecular molecule, no dipole–dipole forces are present.

3. H_2S

The intermolecular forces present in a sample of H_2S are London forces and dipole–dipole forces. London forces are present between all molecules. Dipole–dipole forces are present between polar molecules, and because H_2S is a polar molecule, dipole–dipole forces are present.

HYDROGEN BONDING

Hydrogen bonding is a type of intermolecular force present between molecules containing hydrogen atoms covalently bonded to oxygen, fluorine, or nitrogen. Hydrogen bonding is the strongest of the intermolecular forces. When hydrogen from one molecule is near a highly electronegative atom such as oxygen, fluorine, or nitrogen in another molecule and acts as a bridge between another highly electronegative atom, a hydrogen bond is formed. Hydrogen bonding is responsible for the high boiling point in water and for the crystalline structure of ice.

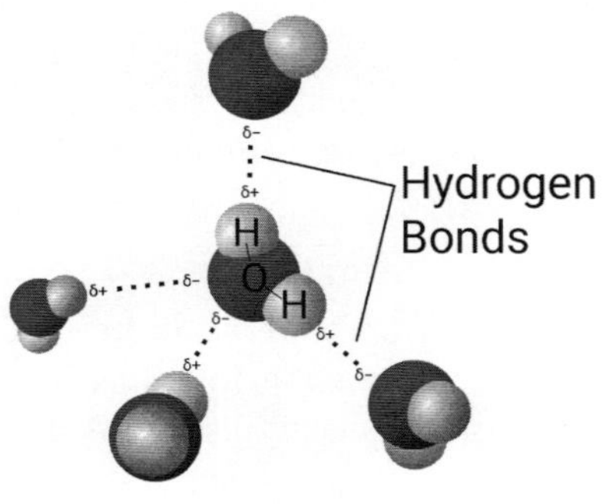

London Forces

London forces are intermolecular forces that exist between all molecules due to the temporary instantaneous dipoles induced by an unequal distribution of electrons around a molecule. London forces are present between all molecules of liquids, solids, and gases. London forces are the weakest of the intermolecular forces and the only intermolecular forces present between nonpolar molecules. London forces are also known as London dispersion forces or dispersion forces. London forces are weaker than both dipole–dipole forces and hydrogen bonds.

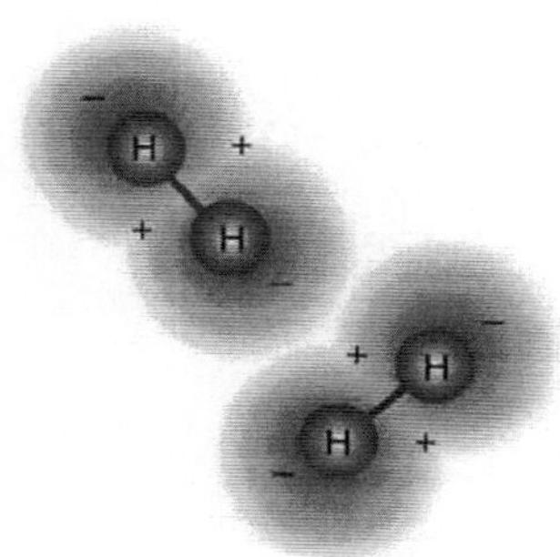

Dipole–Dipole Intermolecular Forces

Dipole–dipole forces are intermolecular forces that occur only between polar molecules. Polar molecules have positive and negative ends because of an unequal sharing of electrons due to the differences in electronegativities between the atoms of the molecules. The positive end of one molecule is attracted to the negative end of the other molecules. Dipole–dipole forces are stronger than London (dispersion) forces but weaker than hydrogen bonds. In the figure below, the dipole–dipole force between the positive end of one hydrogen chloride molecule and the negative end of another hydrogen chloride molecule is indicated by the dashed line.

$$\overset{\delta+}{\text{H}}-\overset{\delta-}{\text{Cl}}\text{- - - -}\overset{\delta+}{\text{H}}-\overset{\delta-}{\text{Cl}}$$

Dipole-Induced Dipole Intermolecular Forces

Whereas dipole–dipole intermolecular forces are between two polar molecules, a dipole-induced intermolecular force is between a polar molecule and a nonpolar molecule. Dipole-induced dipole intermolecular forces are forces that occur when a dipole induces a temporary dipole in a molecule that is nonpolar. The electron cloud of the nonpolar molecule is distorted when it comes near the electron cloud of a dipole. This is typically a weak intermolecular force. However, this dipole-induced dipole intermolecular force is responsible for the stability of hydrates formed from hydrocarbons and some of the noble gases.

Bonding and Structure

Bonding and structure determine whether a substance exists naturally as a solid, liquid, or gas. Properties that are affected by bonding and structure include boiling point, freezing point, and vapor pressure. Bonding and structure determine if a substance is soluble in water or in nonpolar solvents. Also affected are the viscosity of liquids and whether a solid material is hard or soft and whether or not a substance forms crystals or is amorphous. Bonding affects the conductivity of heat and electricity determining if a substance is a good insulator or conductor.

Bonding and structure affect boiling points and melting points. The types of bonds within molecules affect boiling and melting points. Compounds with ionic bonds typically have high melting and boiling points, whereas compounds with covalent bonds typically have low melting and boiling points. Intermolecular forces also affect these points. Substances with hydrogen bonds typically have high boiling and melting points. For example, hydrogen bonds are responsible for the high boiling and melting points of water. For example, the noble gases are indeed all gases.

Bonding and structure affect solubility. The basic idea behind solubility is *like dissolves like.* This means that solutes with polar molecules typically dissolve in solvents with polar molecules. The polarity of the molecules is determined by the type of bonds and the arrangement of those bonds in the molecules. For example, both salt and table sugar (sucrose) dissolve in water because salt, table sugar, and water all have polar molecules. Solutes with nonpolar molecules typically dissolve in solvents with nonpolar molecules. For example, a grease stain will not rinse out with water because water consists of polar molecules due to the asymmetrical arrangement of the polar bonds and grease is a type of lipid that is nonpolar.

Vapor pressure is related to the boiling point of a substance. The boiling point of a substance is the temperature at which the vapor pressure equals the atmospheric pressure. In general, as the vapor pressure increases, the boiling point decreases. Compounds with ionic bonds typically have high boiling points and low vapor pressures. Compounds with covalent bonds typically have low boiling points and high vapor pressures. Substances with the strongest intermolecular forces, hydrogen bonds, typically have high boiling points and low vapor pressures.

Dilute and Concentrated

The terms *dilute* and *concentrated* have opposite meanings. In a solution, the solute is dissolved in the solvent. The more solute that is dissolved, the more concentrated is the solution. The less solute that is dissolved, the less concentrated and the more dilute is the solution. The terms are often associated with the preparation of a stock solution for a laboratory experiment. Stock solutions are typically ordered in a concentrated solution. To prepare for use in a chemistry lab, the stock solutions are diluted to the appropriate molarity by adding a specific amount of solvent such as water to a specific amount of stock solution.

Saturated, Unsaturated, and Supersaturated

The terms *saturated, unsaturated,* and *supersaturated* are associated with solutions. In a solution, a solvent is added to a solvent. In a saturated solution, the solute is added to the solvent until no more solute is able to dissolve. The undissolved solute will settle down to the bottom of the beaker. A solution is considered unsaturated as long as more solute is able to go into solution under ordinary conditions. The solubility of solids in liquids typically increases as temperature increases. If the temperature of a solution is increased as the solute is being added, more solute than is normally possible may go into solution, forming a supersaturated solution.

Mixture, Solution, and Colloid

A **mixture** is made of two or more substances that are combined in various proportions. The exact proportion of the constituents is the defining characteristic of any mixture. There are two types of mixtures: homogeneous and heterogeneous. **Homogeneous** means that the mixture's composition and properties are uniform throughout. Conversely, **heterogeneous** means that the mixture's composition and properties are not uniform throughout.

A **solution** is a homogeneous mixture of substances that cannot be separated by filtration or centrifugation. Solutions are made by dissolving one or more solutes into a solvent. For example, in an aqueous glucose solution, glucose is the solute and water is the solvent. If there is more than one liquid present in the solution, then the most prevalent liquid is considered the solvent. The exact mechanism of dissolving varies depending on the mixture, but the result is always individual solute ions or molecules surrounded by solvent molecules. The proportion of solute to solvent for a particular solution is its **concentration**.

A **colloid** is a heterogeneous mixture in which small particles (<1 micrometer) are suspended, but not dissolved, in a liquid. As such, they can be separated by centrifugation. A commonplace example of a colloid is milk.

Molarity and Molality

Molarity and molality are measures of the concentration of a solution. Molarity (M) is the amount of solute in moles per the amount of solution in liters. A 1.0 M solution consists of 1.0 mole of solute for each 1.0 L of solution. Molality (m) is the amount of solute in moles per the amount of solvent in kilograms. A 1.0 m solution consists of 1.0 mole of solute for each 1.0 kg of solvent. Often, when performing these calculations, the amount of solute is given in grams. To convert from grams of solute to moles of solute, multiply the grams of solute by the molar mass of the solute:

$\text{Molarity (M)} = \frac{\text{moles of solute (mol)}}{\text{liters of solution (L)}}$. $\text{Molality (m)} = \frac{\text{moles of solute (mol)}}{\text{kilograms of solvent (kg)}}$.

Mole Fraction, Parts per Million, Parts per Billion, and Percent by Mass or Volume

Concentrations can be measured in mole fractions, parts per million, parts per billion, and percent by mass or volume. Mole fraction (χ) is calculated by dividing the number of moles of one component by the total number of moles of all of the components of the solution. Parts per million (ppm) is calculated by dividing the mass of the solute in grams by the mass of the solvent and solute in grams and then multiplying the quotient by 1,000,000 ppm. Parts per billion (ppb) is calculated similarly, except the quotient is multiplied by 1,000,000,000 ppb. Percent concentration can be calculated by mass or by volume by dividing the mass or volume of the solute by the mass or volume of the solution. This quotient is a decimal that can be converted to a percent by multiplying by 100.

Calculating Molarity Example

Calculate the molarity of 100.0 g of $CaCl_2$ in 500.0 mL of solution.

To calculate molarity, use the formula molarity (M) = $\frac{\text{moles of solute (mol)}}{\text{liters of solution (L)}}$. The necessary conversions from grams $CaCl_2$ to moles $CaCl_2$ and from 500.0 mL to liters may be performed using dimensional analysis. An alternate method of working this problem would be doing the conversions first and then substituting those values directly into the equation. Using the method of dimensional analysis and substituting the given information into the equation yields molarity = $\frac{100.0 \text{ grams } CaCl_2}{500.0 \text{ mL of solution}}$. Adding the necessary conversions using dimensional analysis yields

$$\text{molarity} = \left(\frac{100.0 \text{ g } CaCl_2}{500.0 \text{ mL of solution}}\right)\left(\frac{\text{mol } CaCl_2}{110.98 \text{ g}}\right)\left(\frac{1000 \text{ mL}}{\text{L}}\right) = 1.802 \text{ M}.$$

Preparing a Dilute Solution from a Stock Solution

In order to prepare a dilute solution from a stock solution, the molarity and the needed volume of the diluted solution as well as the molarity of the stock solution must be known. The volume of the stock solution to be diluted can be calculated using the formula $V_{stock}M_{stock} = V_{dilute}M_{dilute}$, where V_{stock} is the unknown variable, M_{stock} is the molarity of the stock solution, V_{dilute} is the needed volume of the dilute solution, and M_{dilute} is the needed molarity of the dilute solution. Solving this formula for V_{stock} yields $V_{stock} = \frac{V_{dilute}M_{dilute}}{M_{stock}}$. Then, dilute the calculated amount of stock solution (V_{stock}) to the total volume required of the diluted solution.

Effects of Temperature, Pressure, Surface Area, and Agitation on the Dissolution Rate

Temperature, pressure, surface area, and agitation affect the dissolution rate. Increasing the temperature increases the kinetic energy of the molecules, which increases the number of collisions with the solute particles. Increasing the surface area of contact by stirring (agitation) or crushing a solid solute also increases the dissolution rate and helps prevent recrystallization. Increasing the pressure will increase the dissolution rate for gas solutes in liquid solvents because the added pressure will make it more difficult for the gas to escape. Increasing the pressure will have virtually no effect on the dissolution rate for solid solutes in liquid solvents under normal conditions.

Effect of Temperature and Pressure on Solubility

Temperature and pressure affect solubility. For gas solutes in liquid solvents, increasing the temperature increases the kinetic energy causing more gas particles to escape the surface of the liquid solvents and therefore decreasing the solubility of the solutes. For most solid solutes in liquid solvents, increasing the temperature increases the solubility, as shown in this solubility curve for selected salts. For gas solutes in liquid solvents, increasing the pressure increases the solubility.

Increasing the pressure of liquid or solid solutes in liquid solvents has virtually no effect under normal conditions.

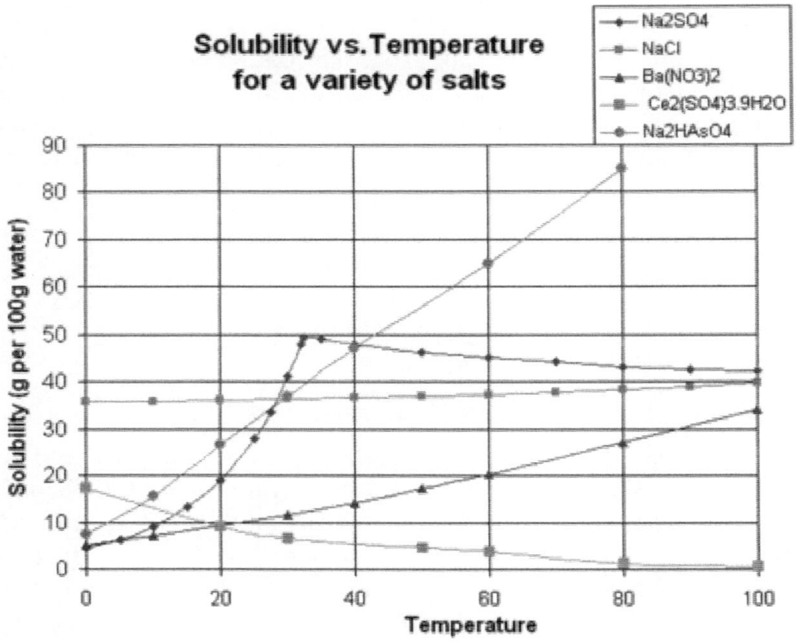

Freezing Point Depression

Freezing point depression is a colligative property of solutions that depends only on the number of particles in solution, not on the identity of those particles. Adding a nonvolatile solute to a solution will lower the freezing point of that solution. This decrease in temperature is known as *freezing point depression*. Basically, the particles of the nonvolatile solute occupy spaces near the surface and block or inhibit the solvent particles from escaping from the surface of the solution. As fewer particles escape, the vapor pressure lowers. This decrease in vapor pressure causes a decrease in the freezing point known as freezing point depression. The amount of depression can be calculated from the equation $\Delta T_{FP} = mk_f$, where m is the molality of the solution and k_f is the molal freezing point constant for that particular solvent.

Boiling Point Elevation

Boiling point elevation is a colligative property of solutions that depends only on the number of particles in solution, not on the identity of those particles. Adding a nonvolatile solute to a solution will raise the boiling point of that solution. This rise in temperature is known as boiling point elevation. Basically, the particles of the nonvolatile solute occupy spaces near the surface and block or inhibit the solvent particles from escaping from the surface of the solution. As fewer particles escape, the vapor pressure lowers. This decrease in vapor pressure causes an increase in the boiling point known as *boiling point elevation*. The amount of elevation can be calculated from the equation $\Delta T_{BP} = mk_b$, where m is the molality of the solution and k_b is the molal boiling point constant for that particular solvent.

Vapor Pressure Lowering

Vapor pressure lowering is a colligative property of solutions that depends only on the number of particles in solution, not on the identity of those particles. Adding a nonvolatile solute to a solution will lower the vapor pressure of that solution. Basically, the particles of the nonvolatile solute occupy spaces near the surface and block or inhibit the solvent particles from escaping from the surface of the solution. As fewer particles escape, the vapor pressure lowers. This decrease in vapor pressure causes an increase in the boiling point and a decrease in the freezing point.

Osmosis

Osmosis can be defined as diffusion through a semipermeable membrane. Typically, small solvent particles can pass through, but larger solute particles are too large to pass through. This means that osmosis is the net flow of solvent from a solution with a lower concentration to a solution with a higher concentration until a state of equilibrium is reached. The pressure that must be applied to the semipermeable membrane to stop the flow of solvent to reach this equilibrium state is called *osmotic pressure*. Osmotic pressure is a colligative property that depends on the number of nonvolatile solute particles, not the identity.

Scientific Inquiry

Formulating a Problem

The first step to scientific inquiry is to formulate the problem. The problem is basically a question that needs to be answered. The problem or question needs to be specific and testable. The problem needs to be interesting, important, and feasible. To fully investigate a problem, an extended experiment or even a series of experiments will need to be performed. In order to develop an adequate problem, the topic to be investigated should be thoroughly researched and studied. Research should include previous experiments performed on the topic and the latest research information available. The problem will define the goal of the scientific inquiry. Without the problem, the researcher cannot proceed. A specific, testable research problem will enable the researcher to formulate a hypothesis and design an experiment. Once formulated, the problem must be stated in concise terms by either posing a question or making a declarative statement.

Forming and Testing a Hypothesis

A hypothesis is a prediction of the outcome of the scientific investigation. In order to form a reasonable hypothesis, a significant amount of observation must first be accomplished followed by a valid problem being stated. A good hypothesis should be a prediction, and it must be testable. A good hypothesis should take into account the available background information on the topic, and it must be able to be proven wrong by a valid test. In chemistry, a valid test of a good hypothesis will typically consist of a controlled experiment that has only one variable and several constants. The test should either prove or disprove the hypothesis.

Experimental research is a valid method of testing a hypothesis. An experiment should be very specific. An experiment should have only one independent variable that is being manipulated to test its effect on one dependent variable. All other factors in the experiment should be held constant. If possible, an experiment should have a control group that verifies that the dependent variable is actually dependent on the independent variable. A good experiment should have sufficient trials. Typically, a good experiment will take many days or several weeks with numerous trials, and each trial should be repeated several times. In a good experiment, the results must be repeatable and measurable.

Model, Theory, and Law

A model is a visual representation that is based on scientific evidence. A model can help scientists attempt to explain information that is difficult to understand or visualize. A model is usually limited to specific conditions. Two examples of models in chemistry are J.J. Thomson's plum pudding model, which represented his view of the atom, and Ernest Rutherford's planetary model of the atom, in which he attempted to explain the way that electrons orbit around the nucleus of an atom.

A theory is an explanation for a pattern that is observed in nature. A theory is supported by scientific evidence and has been verified many times by many different scientists. Two examples of theories in chemistry are the atomic theory of matter and the kinetic theory of matter.

A law is a theory that has been verified multiple times by many researchers over an extended period of time of several years. A theory is accepted to be a valid scientific explanation of a pattern that is observed in nature. Examples of laws in chemistry include the laws of thermodynamics and the gas laws.

OBSERVING, CONCLUDING, AND COMPARING

Observing is using the senses (sight, hearing, touch, smell, and taste) to gather information concerning the topic being investigated. An observation is a fact. Observations should be accurate and objective. Observations can be qualitative or quantitative.

Comparing is listing similarities of objects and events, whereas contrasting is listing differences between objects and events. All measurements such as weight, temperature, and pH are forms of comparing.

Concluding should include reevaluating the hypothesis. Specifically, conclusions should state whether or not the results of the experiment support the hypothesis.

INFERRING, CATEGORIZING, AND GENERALIZING

Inferring involves interpreting observations. Inferring attempts to explain why an observation occurred. Observations are generally considered to be facts, but inferences can be correct or incorrect. Inferences can be logical or illogical depending on the observer. A logical inference should make sense based on the information available from the observations.

Categorizing is organizing information into similar categories. Categorizing involves identifying and classifying information into groups and looking for patterns in those groups or categories.

Generalizing consists of making broad statements concerning the relationship between quantities or concepts. A generalization should apply to most situations but typically does not apply to every situation. Generalizing is a way to sort information into meaningful statements that can be transferred to new situations.

CONTROLS

A valid experiment must be carefully controlled. All variables except the one being testing must be carefully maintained. This means that all conditions must be kept exactly the same except for the independent variable. Additionally, a set of data is usually needed for a control group. The control group represents the "normal" state or condition of the variable being manipulated. Controls can be negative or positive. Positive controls are the variables that the researcher expects to have an effect on the outcome of the experiment. A positive control group can be used to verify that an experiment is set up properly. Negative control groups are typically thought of as placebos. A negative control group should verify that a variable has no effect on the outcome of the experiment. The better an experiment is controlled, the more valid the conclusions from that experiment will be. A researcher is more likely to draw a valid conclusion if all variables other than the one being manipulated are being controlled.

VARIABLES

Every experiment has several variables; however, only one variable should be purposely changed and tested. This variable is the manipulated or independent variable. As this variable is manipulated or changed, another variable, called the responding or dependent variable, is observed and recorded. All other variables in the experiment must be carefully controlled and are usually referred to as constants. For example, when testing the effect of temperature on solubility of a solute, the independent variable is the temperature, and the dependent variable is the solubility. All other factors in the experiment such as pressure, amount of stirring, type of solvent, type of solute, and particle size of the solute are the constants.

Review Video: Identifying Independent and Dependent Variables
Visit mometrix.com/academy and enter code: 627181

Review Video: Percent Yield
Visit mometrix.com/academy and enter code: 565738

Data Collection Planning

A valid experiment must be measurable. Data tables should be formed, and meticulous, detailed data should be collected for every trial. First, the researcher must determine exactly what data are needed and why those data are needed. The researcher should know in advance what will be done with those data at the end of the experimental research. The data should be repeatable, reproducible, and accurate. The researcher should be sure that the procedure for data collection will be reliable and consistent. The researcher should validate the measurement system by performing practice tests and making sure that all of the equipment is correctly calibrated and periodically retesting the procedure and equipment to ensure that all data being collected are still valid.

Scientific Ideas and Change

Scientific ideas are always subject to change. The scientific method includes making observations, forming problems, forming and testing hypotheses, and making conclusions. As new observations are made, new hypotheses are formed. As more accurate methods of testing and better equipment become available, testing hypotheses becomes more and more accurate. Incomplete data, new data, or even improved data may change observations and details previously missed due to faulty assumptions and inadequate equipment and as the improper method and the needed improvements become obvious. With technology always changing, new observations are continually being made, leading to new hypotheses and better ways of testing those hypotheses.

Nature and Scientific Knowledge

The word *science* means knowledge. Science includes knowledge of the natural world. Many scientific fields are divided into categories to study and explain natural phenomena. Observations regarding specific physical evidence are made and then tested. This testing attempts to simulate the observations of nature under controlled conditions. Because natural processes operate in a fairly consistent manner, researchers should be able to identify and predict those patterns. Science is limited: It can only address natural phenomena. Science is testable and should be able to be shown to follow the rules of nature.

Reproducibility

Scientific knowledge should be reproducible. Researchers working independently should be able to repeat experiments and obtain similar results. These results should be commensurate if the setups and the procedures for the experiments are the same. Reproducibility is not the same concept as repeatability. Repeatability is the ability of one researcher to perform numerous trials in one experiment using the same equipment resulting in similar results. Reproducibility is the ability of several researchers to replicate successive experiments under the same conditions but in different locations and with different operators and achieve the same results. Reproducibility indicates that the original experiment was not flawed or inadequate. Reproducibility is completely independent of the original research using different equipment and operators.

Models

A model is a replica or representation of an object or process. Models can look like the actual objects they represent, or models can simply represent the behavior of an object or system while looking quite different. Types of models vary from actual physical objects such as maps and charts to mathematic equations and computer simulations. In chemistry, several models of the atom have been developed over the years. Students can build models of molecular compounds and ionic compounds. Models demonstrating the concepts of diffusing and osmosis are often used. Deoxyribonucleic acid (DNA) is represented by the double-helix model. Gas molecules are modeled with billiard balls or Ping-Pong balls.

Form and Function

The concept of form and function typically fits well with biology. Specifically, the form of an organism or organ is designed in such a way as to perform the required function or functions. For example, red blood cells are designed specifically to perform the function of carrying oxygen. The concept of form and function can also be applied to chemistry. For example, in the area of organic chemistry, carbohydrates, lipids, nucleic acids, and proteins are designed to perform their specific functions. Deoxyribonucleic acid (DNA) and ribonucleic acid (RNA) have different structures that enable them to perform their separate functions. Hundreds of proteins with unique structures have very specific functions in living organisms.

Laboratory Safety Rules

Laboratory safety rules for students should include the following. Never perform unauthorized experiments or work in the laboratory alone. Consider all chemicals to be hazardous unless instructed otherwise. Carefully read the label twice before taking anything from a bottle. Excess reagents are never to be returned to stock bottles. Many common reagents, for example, alcohols and acetone, are highly flammable. Do not use them anywhere near open flames. Always pour acids into water. Avoid skin contact with chemicals. If chemicals come into contact with your skin or eyes, flush immediately with large amounts of water and inform your instructor. Wash your hands at the end of the experiment.

Appropriate Apparel and Conduct

General guidelines for appropriate apparel in the chemistry laboratory are as follows. Safety goggles must be worn at all times while in the laboratory. Wear a chemical-resistant laboratory apron. Roll long sleeves up above the elbow. Closed-toe shoes and long pants must be worn in the lab. Contact lenses are not allowed. Long, loose hair should be tied back. Wear disposable gloves when handling hazardous materials. General guidelines for conduct in the chemistry laboratory are as follows. No practical jokes or boisterous conduct in the laboratory. No horseplay. No eating, drinking, or chewing gum. No unauthorized experiments are to be performed. Never taste anything. Never directly smell the source of any vapor or gas; instead, waft a small sample to your nose. Always wash your hands before leaving the lab.

Appropriate Use of Chemicals in the Laboratory

Chemicals should be used and prepared appropriately in the laboratory. Always weigh potential risk factors of each chemical against the educational value of using the chemical. Know all potential hazards for each chemical. Read every chemical label twice. Instruct students in the use of the Safety Data Sheet (SDS). Never allow students to take chemicals home. Add water to chemicals gently to avoid splashing. Chemicals may be prepared for the laboratory using percentage by weight, percentage by volume, or the molarities of the needed solutions.

Chemicals should be stored in locked cabinets with front-edge lips to prevent accidental spills. These cabinets should be off limits to students. Storage areas should have adequate ventilation. Chemicals should be stored by compatibility first, then alphabetically within those compatibility groups. Acids should be stored in a separate cabinet. Nitric acid must be stored separately from other acids. Flammables should be stored in an approved flammables-storage cabinet. Water-sensitive chemicals should be stored separately in a cool, dry cabinet. Keep chemicals in their original containers, if possible. Label all chemicals that are placed in other containers. Perform a routine inventory of all chemicals. All chemicals should be labeled with the date received and the date opened. Do not store any unlabeled chemicals. Do note store liquids or heavy containers on high shelves. Do not store chemicals on the floor. Purchase and store the chemicals in small quantities only as needed. Do not store any food or drink with any chemicals.

Location of Standard Safety Equipment

Eyewash stations and safety showers should be located less than 10 seconds from the laboratory area, according to Occupational Safety and Health Administration (OSHA) standards. Bottles of eyewash solution should be readily available. If chemicals come into contact with your skin or eyes, flush immediately with large amounts of water. Fire extinguishers should be located according to the building code. Fire blankets should be readily available. Fire blankets may be used to smother small fires. Never use a carbon dioxide extinguisher on a person.

Appropriate Use and Storage of Laboratory Equipment

Laboratory equipment should be used properly. Never leave burners unattended. Turn off burners if you leave your workstation. Be sure that the gas is shut off when you leave the lab. Never point a test tube that you are heating at yourself or your lab partner. Beware of hot glass. Never use chipped or broken glassware. Clean up all broken glassware immediately, and dispose of the broken glass properly. Do not use broken or unsafe equipment. Use Pyrex glassware when heating materials. Use plastic substitutes for glassware as appropriate.

Safe Disposal of Materials

The safe disposal of materials in the laboratory should include a minimum of the following. Check the Safety Data Sheet (SDS) for the correct disposal procedure for each chemical. Check with local authorities concerning possible restrictions before disposing of materials. Do not pour chemicals down the drain unless approved by local authorities. Usually, dilute solutions of inorganic salts, in which neither ion is highly acidic or basic, are approved for drainage disposal. Some organics may be flushed down the drain with large amounts of water. Use professional waste haulers for all hazardous waste. Provide appropriate waste containers. Properly dispose of unwanted chemicals. Treat spills properly.

Standard Emergency Procedures

Standard emergency procedures for the student in the chemistry laboratory should include the following. Always notify the instructor of any type of emergency. In the event of possible exposure to chemicals with the eyes or the skin, use eye-wash stations, the sink, or the safety shower as necessary. If necessary, seek medical attention. Be aware of the locations of fire evacuation routes, fire extinguishers, and fire blankets. In the event of a fire, pull the fire alarm. In the event of an evacuation, if possible, turn off all gas and remove chemicals from heat sources. In cases of ingestion, call a poison control center.

Practice Test #1

1. Three liquids, X, Y and Z are placed in separate flasks, each of which is suspended in a water bath at 75 °C. The boiling points of each liquid are

X, 273 K
Y, 340 K
Z, 360 K

Which of the three liquids will begin to boil after warming to 75 °C?

a. X, Y, and Z
b. X and Z
c. X and Y
d. Y and Z

2. One mole of an ideal gas is compressed to 10 L and heated to 25 °C. What is the pressure of the gas?

Please provide your answer on the supplied griddable sheet.

3. Determine the oxidation states of each of the elements in $KMnO_4$:

a. K^{+1}, Mn^{+7}, O^{-8}
b. K^{-1},Mn^{+7}, O^{-2}
c. K^{+1}, Mn^{+3}, O^{-4}
d. K^{+1}, Mn^{+7},O^{-2}

4. Which of the following radioactive emissions results in an increase in atomic number?

a. Alpha
b. Negative Beta
c. Positive Beta
d. Gamma

5. 1 mole of water and 1 mole of argon are in a cylinder at 110 °C and 1 atm of pressure. The temperature of the cylinder is reduced to -5 °C. Which statement about the contents of the cylinder is most accurate?

a. The pressure in the cylinder is decreased, and the partial pressure of argon is less than that of water.
b. The pressure in the cylinder is about the same, and the partial pressure of water is less than that of argon.
c. The pressure in the cylinder is decreased, and the partial pressure of water is much less than that of argon.
d. The pressure in the cylinder is decreased and the partial pressure of water is the same as argon.

6. A liquid is heated from 50 °C to 80 °C. Which of the following statements is generally true about the solubility of solids and gases in the liquid?

a. The solubility of solids will increase and the solubility of gases will decrease
b. The solubility of solids will decrease and the solubility of gases will increase
c. The solubility of solids will increase and the solubility of gases will increase
d. The solubility of solids will decrease and the solubility of gases will decrease

7. Describe the correct outer shell electronic arrangement of phosphorous.

a. $4s^2\ 4p^3$
b. $3s^2\ 3p^3$
c. $2s^2\ 3p^3$
d. $2s^2\ 2p^3$

8. Arrange the following compounds from most polar to least polar:

F_2, CH_3CH_2Cl, NaCl, CH_3OH

a. NaCl>CH_3OH> CH_3CH_2Cl> F_2
b. F_2> NaCl> CH_3OH>CH_3CH_2Cl
c. CH_3OH>NaCl>F_2>CH_3CH_2Cl
d. NaCl>F_2>CH_3OH>CH_3CH_2Cl

9. A solid is heated until it melts. Which of the following is true about the solid melting?

a. ΔH is positive, and ΔS is positive
b. ΔH is negative and ΔS is positive
c. ΔH is positive and ΔS is negative
d. ΔH is negative and ΔS is negative

10. A liquid is held at its freezing point and slowly allowed to solidify. Which of the following statements about this event are true?

a. During freezing, the temperature of the material decreases
b. While freezing, heat is given off by the material
c. During freezing, heat is absorbed by the material
d. During freezing, the temperature of the material increases

11. Which of the following is an incorrect Lewis structure?

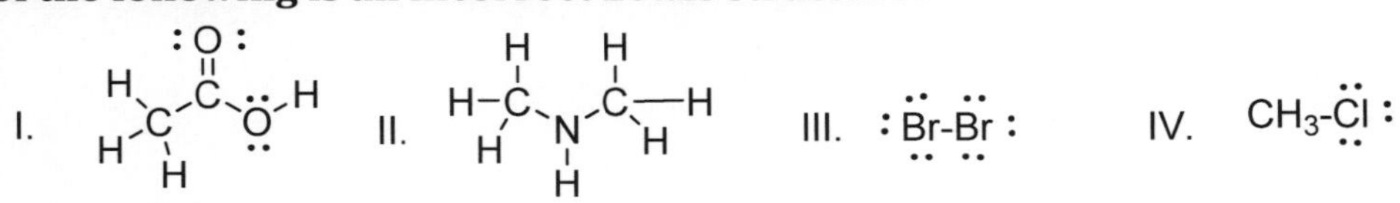

a. I
b. II
c. III
d. IV

12. Hund's rule regarding electronic configuration states:

a. Electrons in the same orbital must have an opposite spin
b. Electrons must fill lower energy orbitals before filling higher energy orbitals
c. Electrons must populate empty orbitals of equal energy before filling occupied orbitals
d. Electrons must have the same nuclear spin as the nucleus

13. 100 g of ethanol C_2H_6O is dissolved in 100 g of water. The final solution has a volume of 0.2 L. What is the density of the resulting solution?

a. 0.5 g/mL
b. 1 g/mL
c. 46 g/mL
d. 40 g/mL

14. Gas X is in a cylinder at 1 atm of pressure and has a volume of 10 L at 0° C. Gas X spontaneously decomposes to gas Y, according to the equation

$$X \longrightarrow 3Y$$

The temperature in the cylinder remains the same during the reaction. What is the pressure in the cylinder now?

a. 1 atm
b. 3 atm
c. 4 atm
d. Cannot be determined

15. Determine the number of neutrons, protons and electrons in ^{238}U.

a. 238, 92, 238
b. 92, 146, 146
c. 146, 92, 92
d. 92, 92, 146

16. Arrange the following elements in order of increasing atomic radius:

a. K<Zn<Fe<As<Kr
b. K<Fe<Zn<Kr<As
c. Kr<As<Fe<K<Zn
d. Kr<As<Zn<Fe<K

17. What is the mass of 2.00 liters of a sugar solution with a density of 1.15 g/ml?

a. 2.30 kg
b. 0.023 kg
c. 1.15 kg
d. 0.58 kg

18. Comparing pure water and a 1 M aqueous solution of NaCl, both at 1 atm of pressure, which of the following statements is most accurate?

a. The pure water will boil at a higher temperature, and be less conductive
b. The pure water will boil at a lower temperature and be less conductive
c. The pure water will boil at a lower temperature and be more conductive
d. The pure water boil at the same temperature and be more conductive

19. Which bond has the shortest length?

a. sp^2
b. sp^3
c. sp
d. pi

20. A material has a half life of 2 years. If you started with 1 kg of the material, how much would be left after 8 years?

Please provide your answer on the supplied griddable sheet.

21. Silver nitrate ($AgNO_3$) is dissolved in water. One drop of an aqueous solution containing NaCl is added and almost instantly, a white milky precipitate forms. What is the precipitate?

a. NaCl
b. $NaNO_3$
c. $AgNO_3$
d. AgCl

22. Determine the heat of combustion for the following reaction:

$$Propane + 5\ O_2 \rightarrow 3\ CO_2 + 4\ H_2O$$

The standard heats of formation for propane, CO_2 and water are -103.8 KJ/mol, -393.5 KJ/mol and -285.8 KJ/mol respectively.

a. -2220 KJ/mol
b. -2323.7 kJ/mol
c. 2220 KJ/mol
d. 2323.7 KJ/mol

23. The best way to separate isotopes of the same element is to exploit:

a. Differences in chemical reactivity
b. Differences in reduction potential
c. Differences in toxicity
d. Differences in mass

24. What is the chemical composition of ammonium sulfate?

a. N 21%, H 3%, S 24%, O 32%
b. N 10%, H 6%, S 24%, O 60%
c. N 10%, H 4%, S 12%, O 74%
d. N 21%, H 6%, S 24%, O 48%

25. If the reaction shown below is exothermic, the energy level of the reactants is

$$H_2 + O_2 \rightarrow 2\ H_2O$$

a. lower than that of the products.
b. higher than the activation energy of the reaction.
c. possibly lower, possibly higher than that of the products.
d. higher than that of the products.

26. An alpha particle consists of

a. Two electrons and two protons
b. Two electrons and two neutrons
c. Four neutrons
d. Two protons and two neutrons

27. Place the following in the correct order of increasing acidity.

a. $HCl < HF < HI < HBr$
b. $HCl < HBr < HI < HF$
c. $HI < HBr < HCl < HF$
d. $HF < HCl < HBr < HI$

28. Balance the following reaction between sulfuric acid and aluminum hydroxide by filling in the correct stoichiometric values for each chemical.

_ H_2SO_4 + _ $Al(OH)_3$ → _ $Al_2(SO_4)_3$ + _ H_2O

a. 3, 2, 1, 6
b. 2, 3, 1, 3
c. 3, 3, 2, 6
d. 1, 2, 1, 4

29. Which of the following statements is true about the physical properties of liquids and gases?

I. Liquids and gases are both compressible
II. Liquids flow, but gases do not
III. Liquids flow, and gases are incompressible
IV. Liquids flow and gases are compressible
V. Gases flow and liquids are incompressible

a. I and III
b. II and IV
c. III and V
d. IV and V

30. Calculate the mass of water produced from the reaction of 1 kg of n-heptane with oxygen.

n-heptane (1 kg) + 11 O_2 → 7 CO_2 + 8 H_2O

Please provide your answer on the supplied griddable sheet.

31. The primary substances of which all other things are composed are

a. protons.
b. compounds.
c. electrons.
d. elements.

32. 50 grams of acetic acid $C_2H_4O_2$ are dissolved in 200 g of water. Calculate the weight % and mole fraction of the acetic acid in the solution.

a. 20%, 0.069
b. 0.069%, 0.20
c. 25%, 0.075
d. 20%, 0.075

33. Magnesium metal is reacted with hydrobromic acid according to the following equation:

$Mg + 2HBr \rightarrow MgBr_2 + H_2$

If 100 g of Mg is reacted with 100 g of HBr, which statement about the reaction is true?

a. Mg is the limiting reagent
b. HBr is the excess reagent
c. Mg is the excess reagent
d. 100 g of $MgBr_2$ will be produced

34. When a solid is heated and transforms directly to the gaseous phases, this process is called:

a. sublimation
b. fusion
c. diffusion
d. condensation

35. Which of the following reactions produces products with higher entropy than the starting materials?

I. Glucose (s) + water →glucose (aq)
II. 4Al (s) + $3O_2$(g)→$2Al_2O_3$(s)
III. Br_2 + light→2 Br
IV. Ice →water vapor

a. II, III
b. I, II
c. I, III
d. I, III, IV

36. What is the mass number of an atom of potassium that has 20 neutrons?

a. 39
b. 15
c. 35
d. 59

37. Place the following in the correct order of increasing solubility in water.

a. Butanol<ethanol<octane<NaCl
b. Ethanol<NaCl<octane<butanol
c. NaCl<octane<butanol<ethanol
d. Octane<butanol<ethanol<NaCl

38. The overall reaction A→D can be described by the following equation:

$$A \xrightarrow{\text{fast}} B \xrightarrow{\text{slow}} C \xrightarrow{\text{fast}} D$$

What would be the rate law for the overall reaction of A to D?

a. Rate = k[D]/[A]
b. Rate = k[B]
c. Rate = [B]
d. Rate = k[C]/[B]

39. How many electrons are in the atom ${}^{45}_{20}Ca$?

a. 20
b. 45
c. 65
d. 25

40. A 10 L cylinder contains 4 moles of oxygen, 3 moles of nitrogen and 7 moles of neon. The temperature of the cylinder is increased from 20 °C to 40 °C. Determine the partial pressure of neon in the cylinder as a percentage of the whole.

Please provide your answer on the supplied griddable sheet.

41. How many protons are in an isotope of sodium with a mass number of 25?

a. 11
b. 14
c. 15
d. 32

42. Which of the following molecules are alkenes?

I. 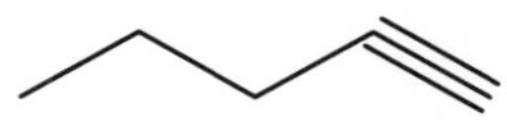

II. 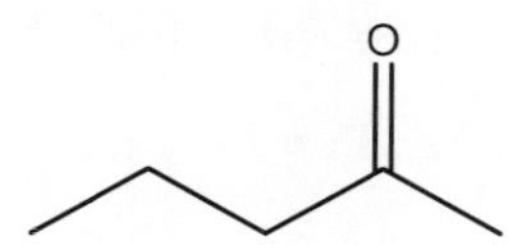

III. 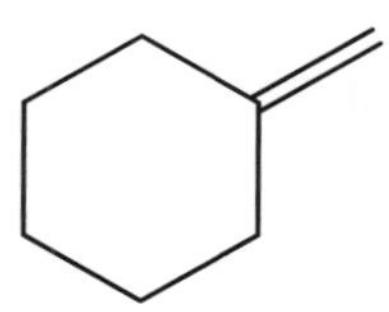

IV. 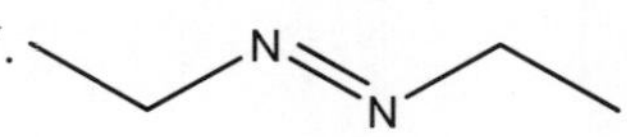

a. I
b. II
c. III
d. IV

43. Which of the following elements would likely be good reducing agents?

a. Br_2
b. N_2
c. Na
d. Ne

44. Any reaction that absorbs 150 kcal of energy can be classified as

a. activated.
b. exothermic.
c. oxidation.
d. endothermic.

45. An anion always

a. forms covalent bonds.
b. contains a group of two or more atoms with a positive charge.
c. has a negative charge.
d. has a positive charge.

46. Which of the following statements generally describes the trend of electronegativity considering the Periodic Table of the Elements?

a. Electronegativity increases going from left to right and from top to bottom
b. Electronegativity increases going from right to left and from bottom to top
c. Electronegativity increases going from left to right and from bottom to top
d. Electronegativity increases going from right to left and from top to bottom

47. Ammonium Phosphate $(NH_4)_3PO_4$ is a strong electrolyte. What will be the concentration of all the ions in a 0.9 M solution of ammonium phosphate?

a. 0.9 M NH_4^+, 0.9 M PO_4^{3-}
b. 0.3 M NH_4^+, 0.9 M PO_4^{3-}
c. 2.7 M NH_4^+, 0.9 M PO_4^{3-}
d. 2.7 M NH_4^+, 2.7 M PO_4^{3-}

48. What is the correct formula for a compound formed from the elements aluminum (Al) and oxygen (O)?

a. AlO
b. Al_2O_3
c. Al_3O_2
d. AlO_3

49. What is the electron level arrangement for aluminum?

a. 2,8,5
b. 2,8,8
c. 2,8,10
d. 2,8,3

50. 100 g of H_3PO_4 is dissolved in water, producing 400 mL of solution. What is the normality of the solution?

Please provide your answer on the supplied griddable sheet.

51. Which scientist was responsible for developing the format of the modern periodic table?

a. Faraday
b. Einstein
c. Hess
d. Mendeleev

52. Which of the following molecules is named correctly?

(A) 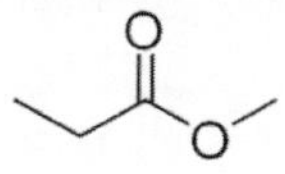

methyl propionate

(B) 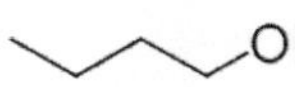

1-propanol

(C) 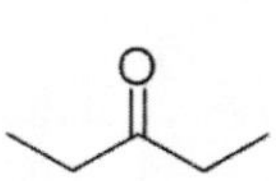

3-propanoic acid

(D) 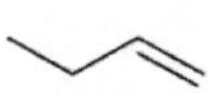

3-butene

Answers and Explanations

1. C: To convert from degrees Celsius to Kelvin, add 273. 75° C is equivalent to 348 K. Both X and Y have lower boiling points, which means that they will each boil in the water bath. Z will never become warm enough to boil.

2. 2.4 atm: Plugging the data into the ideal gas law using the correct units gives the correct answer in atmospheres, which in this case is 2.4 atm. The equation is P = nRT/V. So we have P = 1 mol (0.08206 L atm/mol K)(298 K)/10 L. The R value is 0.08206 L atm/mol K when using L as the volume unit, and delivers the pressure in atm.

3. D: Each oxygen has a charge of -2 for a total negative charge of -8. Potassium (K) only exists in compounds as +1. Therefore for the molecule to have a neutral charge, the Mn must be in a +7 oxidation state.

4. B: Negative beta emission represents the spontaneous decay of a neutron into a proton with the release of an electron. Therefore the resulting nucleus will have one more proton than it did before the reaction, and protons represent the atomic number of an atom. Alpha decay results in the emission of a helium nucleus. The resulting nucleus of an alpha decay would lose two protons and two neutrons, causing a decrease in both the atomic number and the mass number. Gamma decay does not affect the numbers of protons or neutrons in the nucleus. It is an emission of a photon, or packet of energy.

5. C: As the temperature drops to -5 °C, the water vapor condenses to a liquid, and then to a solid. The vapor pressure of a solid is much less than that of the corresponding gas. The argon is still a gas at -5 °C, so almost all the pressure in the cylinder is due to argon.

6. A: The higher the temperature of the liquid, the greater the solubility of the solid, while the higher the temperature, the lower the solubility of the gas.

7. B: Phosphorus is in the third period, so the outermost levels must be 3s, 3p. Phosphorus is in Group 5A, which indicates that it has 5 valence electrons. To fill the 3s and 3p, 2 electrons first fill the s orbital, and then the remaining 3 electrons enter the p orbitals. So, $3s^2\ 3p^3$.

8. A: NaCl is an ionic salt, and therefore the most polar. F_2 is nonpolar since the two atoms share the electrons in an equal and symmetrical manner. CH_3OH is an alcohol with a very polar O-H bond. CH_3CH_2Cl is also a polar molecule due to the unequal sharing of electrons between in the C-Cl bond.

9. A: Heat is absorbed by the solid during melting, therefore ΔH is positive. Going from a solid to a liquid greatly increases the freedom of the particles, therefore increasing the entropy, so ΔS is also positive.

10. B: Freezing is an exothermic event; therefore heat must be given off. The temperature of the material remains unchanged at the freezing point during the process.

11. B: The nitrogen is missing its lone pair of electrons, and should have two dots above it. A correct Lewis structure shows how the atoms are connected to each other as well as all of the valence electrons in the compound. Each bond represents two electrons.

12. C: Hund's rule states that electrons must populate empty orbitals of similar energy before pairing up. The Aufbau principle states that electrons must fill lower energy orbitals before filling higher energy orbitals. The Pauli exclusion principle states that no two electrons in the same atom can have the same four quantum numbers, and therefore, two electrons in the same orbital will have opposite spins.

13. B: Density is determined by dividing the mass of the solution by its volume. The mass is 200 g, and the total volume is 0.2 L, or 200 mL. So 200 g/200 mL = 1 g/mL.

14. B: Since both the volume and the temperature remain fixed, the only variable that changes is the number of moles of particles. Because there are now 3 times as many particles as there were originally, the pressure must increase proportionately and so the pressure must be 3 atm.

15. C: The mass number is the number of protons and the number of neutrons added together. The number of protons is also known as the atomic number and can be found on the periodic table. Therefore, the number of neutrons is the mass number (238) less the number of protons, in this case, 92, so we have 146 neutrons. The number of electrons always equals the number of protons in a neutral atom, so C is the correct answer.

16. D: All of the elements belong to the same row in the periodic table. Atomic radii increase going from right to left in any row of the periodic table. Although these elements belonged to the same row, it is important to also know that atomic radii increase from top to bottom in the groups of the periodic table.

17. A: Given that 1 liter (L) corresponds to 1000 milliliters and 1 kilogram (kg) is equivalent to 1000 grams (g), the mass of the solution can be calculated as follows:

$$(2000\text{ ml}) \times (1.15\text{ g/ml}) = (2000\ \cancel{\text{ml}}) \times (1.15\text{ g/}\cancel{\text{ml}}) = 2300\text{ g} = 2.3\text{ kg}$$

18. B: Pure water boils at 100 °C. Water that has salts dissolved in it will boil at a slightly higher temperature, and will conduct electricity much better than pure water.

19. C: The more s character the bond has, the shorter it will be. A triple bond is stronger and shorter than a double bond, which is stronger and shorter than a single bond. An sp orbital is found in a triple bond. An sp^2 orbital is found in a double bond and sp^3 orbitals are found in single bonds.

20. 0.06 kg: Since each half life is 2 years, eight years would be 4 half lives. So the mass of material is halved 4 times. Therefore if we start with 1 kg, at two years we would have 0.5 kg, at four years we would have 0.25 kg, after 6 years we would have 0.12 kg, and after 8 years we would have 0.06 kg.

21. D: $AgNO_3$, $NaNO_3$ and NaCl are all highly water soluble and would not precipitate under these conditions. All nitrate compounds and compounds containing Group I metals are soluble in water. AgCl is essentially insoluble in water, and this is the precipitate observed.

22. A: The heat of combustion is determined by subtracting the heats of formation of the reactants from that of the products. So 3(-393.5) + 4(-285.8) – (-103.8) = -2220.

23. D: Isotopes of the same element must have the same chemical behavior, so A, B, and C all represent, in one form or another, chemical behavior. Isotopes differ in mass, and this can be used to separate them by some appropriate physical property.

24. D: The correct structure of ammonium sulfate is $(NH_4)_2SO_4$. Its molecular weight is 132. The masses of the elements in the compound are: nitrogen 28 (2 x 14), hydrogen 8 (1x8), sulfur 32 (32x1) and oxygen 64 (16x4). To find the percentage composition of each element, divide the element mass by the molecular weight of the compound. So nitrogen is (28/132) = 21%, hydrogen is (8/132) = 6%, sulfur is (32/132) = 24%, and oxygen is (64/132) = 48%.

25. D: In an exothermic reaction, heat is generated when the reactants give rise to product. In such reactions, the reactants have a higher energy level. The energy released, or the heat of reaction, corresponds to the difference in energy level between the reactants and the reaction products.

26. D: An alpha particle is a helium nucleus, which contains two protons and two neutrons.

27. D: Acidity increases as we travel down the periodic table with regard to the halogens. Even though fluorine is the most electronegative element and would be expected to stabilize a negative charge well, it is such a small atom that it is poorly able to stabilize the negative charge and therefore will have a stronger bond to the hydrogen. As the atoms get larger, moving from fluorine to iodine, the ability to stabilize a negative charge becomes greater and the bond with the hydrogen is weaker. A stronger bond with the between the halogen and the hydrogen will result in less acidity, since fewer hydrogen ions will be produced.

28. A: By comparing the products to the reactants, there must be at least two Al atoms in the starting material, and at least three sulfate groups. Therefore, a coefficient of 2 must be placed in front of $Al(OH)_3$ and a coefficient of 3 must be placed in front of H_2SO_4. To make the number of hydrogen and oxygen atoms equal on both sides of the equation, a coefficient of 6 must be placed in front of H_2O.

29. D: Both liquids and gases are fluids and therefore flow, but only gases are compressible. The molecules that make up a gas are very far apart, allowing the gas to be compressed into a smaller volume.

30. 1.4 kg: 1 kg of heptane (MW 100) is equal to 10 moles of heptane. Since 8 moles of water is produced for every mole of heptane reacted, 80 moles of water must be produced. 80 moles of water (MW 18) equals 1440 g, or 1.4 kg.

31. D: Protons and electrons are constituents of atoms. The precise numbers of protons, electrons, and neutrons in an atom define the various elements which can combine to form compounds and molecules.

32. A: The weight % of the acetic acid is the mass of acetic acid divided by the mass of the acetic acid plus the water. So 50g/(50g +200g) = 0.2, or 20%. The mole fraction is the moles of acetic acid divided by the total number of moles of the solution. So 50 g of acetic acid (MW = 60) is 50g/ 60 g/mol = 0.83 moles. 200 g of water = 11.11 moles. Therefore, 0.83 mol/(0.83 mol + 11.11 mol) = 0.069.

33. C: 100 g of HBr equals 1.23 moles, and 100 g of Mg equals 4.11 moles. From the coefficients of the balanced equation, the ratio of HBr to Mg is 2:1. This means that to react 1.23 moles of HBr, 2.46 moles of Mg would be required. Since 4.11 moles of Mg are present, Mg is in excess.

34. A: Sublimation is the process of a solid changing directly into a gas without entering the liquid phase. Fusion refers to a liquid turning into a solid. Diffusion is the process of a material dispersing throughout another. Condensation is generally a gas turning into a liquid.

35. D: In I, dissolving a solid into a liquid breaks up the organized solid matrix, therefore increasing disorder. III converts single particles into two particles, and in IV, solid ice sublimes into a gas.

Both of these processes also increase disorder and thus, entropy. II is a decrease in entropy, since 7 molecules, with 3 being gaseous, are reacted to form 2 solid molecules.

36. A: The mass number of an element is defined as the number of protons (atomic number) plus the number of neutrons in the nucleus. The atomic number of potassium is 19, so there are 19 protons. If the atom of potassium has 20 neutrons, the mass number would be 20 + 19, or 39.

37. D: Octane is a nonpolar hydrocarbon with little or no water solubility. Butanol is an alcohol with a small amount of solubility due to its polar –OH group. Ethanol is a smaller, more polar alcohol that is very soluble in water. NaCl is an ionic salt that is highly soluble in water.

38. B: Since the conversion of B to C is the slow step, this is the only one that determines the reaction rate law. Therefore, the rate law will be based on B, since it is the only reactant in producing C.

39. A: Since the atomic number is 20, which represents the number of protons in the atom, there must be an equal number of electrons in a neutral atom. Protons have a positive charge and electrons are negative. Equal numbers of protons and electrons will result in a neutral atom, or zero charge.

40. 50% of the total pressure: Since there are 7 moles of neon out of a total of 14 moles of gas in the cylinder, the partial pressure of neon will always be 50% of the total pressure, regardless of the temperature.

41. A: The mass number of an element is defined as the number of protons (atomic number) plus the number of neutrons in the nucleus. The atomic number of sodium is 11, so there are 11 protons in the nucleus of all isotopes of sodium. In this case, where the mass number is 25, there must be 14 neutrons (25 – 11) in the isotope of sodium.

42. C: The first is an alkyne, which contains a triple bond between carbon atoms. The second is a ketone and contains a carbon-oxygen double bond. The third is an alkene, which has a double bond between two carbon atoms. The fourth is an imide, which contains a double bond between two nitrogen atoms.

43. C: Reducing agents give up electrons to another chemical species, which cause that species to gain an electron and become reduced. Oxidizing agents cause another species to be oxidized, or to lose an electron, and are themselves reduced as they gain that electron. Bromine is very electronegative, and is almost always an oxidizing agent. N_2 is nearly inert, or unreactive. Neon is an inert noble gas and would not be a reducing agent. Sodium (Na) is very reactive and eager to give up an electron, and is therefore a good reducing agent in a wide variety of reactions.

44. D: Reactions that require energy are termed endothermic, as opposed to those where the reaction generates heat and are designated exothermic. These terms refer solely to the heat of reaction and not the mechanism of the reaction.

45. C: An anion is a molecule that has gained electrons to gain a net negative charge. An anion can be composed of more than one atom but always has a net negative charge. Anions participate in ionic bonds.

46. C: The most electronegative atoms are found near the top right of the periodic table. Fluorine has a high electronegativity, while Cesium, located near the bottom left of the table, has a low electronegativity.

47. C: Since there are three moles of NH_4^+ per mole of salt and 1 mole of PO_4^{3-} per mole of salt, the total ionic concentrations must be 2.7 M of NH_4^+, and 0.9 M of PO_4^{3-}.

48. B: Aluminum (atomic number = 13) has a valence of 3^+ since there are only three electrons in its highest energy level (2,8,3). Oxygen (atomic number = 8) has a valence of 2^- since six electrons are found in the second energy level, which can hold eight electrons. Therefore, to form a compound that is neutral and where the highest energy level is filled would require three atoms of aluminum and two atoms of oxygen:

$$(2 \times -3) + (3 \times -2) = 0$$

49. D: The atomic number of aluminum is 13. This means that the number of protons is 13. Therefore, in a neutral aluminum atom, there are 13 electrons. The first energy level of an atom can hold two electrons. The second and third can each hold eight electrons. In the case of aluminum, this means that the second energy level would be filled, leaving three electrons to occupy the third energy level (13 – 2 – 8 = 3).

50. 7.65 N: Normality refers to the concentration of acid equivalents (H^+ ions), not the concentration of the solute. 100 g of phosphoric acid has a MW of 98 g/mol. So, 100g/98 g/mol = 1.02 moles of phosphoric acid are in solution. The total volume of the solution is 0.4 L, so the molarity of the solution is 1.02 mol/0.4 L = 2.55 M. Since there are three acid equivalents for every mole of phosphoric acid, the normality is 3 x 2.55 = 7.65 N.

51. D: Mendeleev was able to connect the trends of the different elements' behaviors and develop a table that showed the periodicity of the elements and their relationship to each other.

52. A: B is 1-butanol, since its longest chain of carbons is 4, not 3. C is 3-pentanone, since there are 5 carbons in the chain and it is a ketone, rather than a carboxylic acid. D is 1-butene, not 3-butene. The name should be assigned by giving the double bond the lowest number.

Practice Test #2

1. Which of the following actions would increase the freezing point of a solution?

I. Divide the solution into two separate containers.
II. Heat the solution to boil off some of the solvent.
III. Initiate a reaction that causes some of the solute to precipitate.

a. I and II
b. II
c. III
d. I and III

2. A gas at constant volume is cooled. Which statement about the gas must be true?

a. The kinetic energy of the gas molecules has decreased.
b. The gas has condensed to a liquid.
c. The weight of the gas has decreased.
d. The density of the gas has increased.

3. Which substance is most likely to be a solid at STP?

a. Kr
b. Na
c. NH_3
d. Xe

4. In an electron dot structure of an element, the dots are used to represent only the electrons that will participate in bond formation.

a. the valence electrons.
b. the electrons that the element will gain when it forms a compound.
c. all of the electrons in the atom.
d. the electron arrangement.

5. Which is the correct order of increasing intermolecular attractive forces?

a. Dipole-dipole<ionic<hydrogen bonding<London dispersion
b. Ionic<dipole-dipole<London dispersion<hydrogen bonding
c. Hydrogen bonding<London dispersion<ionic<dipole-dipole
d. London dispersion<dipole-dipole<hydrogen bonding<ionic

6. Which of the following represents the correct increasing order of acidity?

a. $CH_3COOH<CH_3OH<CH_3CH_3<HCl$
b. $CH_3CH_3<CH_3OH<CH_3COOH<HCl$
c. $CH_3CH_3<CH_3COOH<CH_3OH<HCl$
d. $CH_3OH<CH_3CH_3<HCl<CH_3COOH$

7. Which of the following compounds contains an ionic bond?

a. H_2O
b. H_2
c. CaO
d. CH_4

8. To make a good buffering system in the pH range of 5-9, which acid/base combinations would likely work the best?

a. HCl/NaOH
b. $HNO_3/NaNO_3$
c. $H_2SO_4/NaHSO_4$
d. NaH_2PO_4/Na_2HPO_4

9. One mole of oxygen gas and two moles of hydrogen are combined in a sealed container at STP. Which of the following statements is true?

a. The mass of hydrogen gas is greater than the mass of oxygen.
b. The volume of hydrogen is greater than the volume of oxygen.
c. The hydrogen and oxygen will react to produce two moles of water.
d. The partial pressure of hydrogen is greater than the partial pressure of oxygen.

10. The precision of a number of data points refers to:

a. How accurate the data is
b. How many errors the data contains
c. How close the data points are to the mean of the data
d. How close the actual data is to the predicted result

11. Ionization energy is

a. highest for metals in Group IA.
b. the energy needed to remove the least tightly bound electron.
c. the energy an ion acquires from an electron.
d. higher for potassium than lithium.

12. The O-H bond in water is polar because

a. it is an ionic bond.
b. it is a hydrogen bond.
c. oxygen is much more electronegative than hydrogen.
d. oxygen occupies more space than hydrogen.

13. One liter of a 0.02 M solution of methanol in water is prepared. What is the mass of methanol in the solution, and what is the approximate molality of methanol?

a. 0.64 g, 0.02 m
b. 0.32 g, 0.01 m
c. 0.64 g, 0.03 m
d. 0.32 g, 0.02 m

14. For the conversion of water into steam, which of the following is true?

a. $\Delta T=0, \Delta S>0$
b. $\Delta T>0, \Delta S = 0$
c. $\Delta T =0, \Delta S <0$
d. $\Delta T >0, \Delta S >0$

15. Which of the following is a characteristic of the modern periodic table?

a. The A groups contain the transition elements.
b. A group is a horizontal row on the periodic table.
c. A period is a column on the periodic table.
d. The elements in each group have similar chemical properties.

16. In the reaction of silver nitrate ($AgNO_3$) with sodium chloride (NaCl), how many grams of silver chloride (AgCl) will be produced from 100 grams of silver nitrate when it is mixed with an excess of sodium chloride? The equation for the reaction is as follows:

$$AgNO_3 + NaCl \rightarrow AgCl + NaNO_3$$

Please provide your answer on the supplied griddable sheet.

17. What is the correct IUPAC name of the compound Fe_2O_3?

a. Iron (I) oxide
b. Iron (II) oxide
c. Iron (III) oxide
d. Iron (IV) oxide

18. The octet rule indicates that

a. all of the Group A elements have eight valence electrons.
b. the noble gases react with other compounds to get eight valence electrons.
c. all of the shells in an atom hold a maximum of eight electrons.
d. atoms lose, gain, or share valence electrons to have eight valence electrons.

19. The ability of an atom to attract the shared electrons in a covalent bond is its

a. nonpolarity.
b. bonding ability.
c. polarity.
d. electronegativity.

20. C-14 has a half life of 5730 years. If you started with 1 mg of C-14 today, how much would be left in 20,000 years?

Please provide your answer on the supplied griddable sheet.

21. Which of the following are considered Lewis acids?

I. H_2SO_4
II. $AlCl_3$
III. PCl_3
IV. $FeCl_3$

a. II and IV
b. II and III
c. I and IV
d. I and II

22. Graham's law is best used to determine what relationship between two different materials?

a. pressure and volume
b. volume and temperature
c. mass and diffusion rate
d. Diffusion rate and temperature

23. Elements in group IIA(2) of the periodic table form ions with a charge of

a. 3^+
b. 0
c. 1^-
d. 2^+

24. In a covalently bonded molecule, the number of electrons that an atom shares with others is usually equal to the number of electrons

a. in the atom.
b. in all the atoms.
c. in its ion.
d. needed to give a noble gas arrangement.

25. 100 g of NH_3 are cooled from 100 °C to 25 °C. What is the heat change for this transition? The heat capacity of ammonia gas is 35.1 J/(mol) (°K)

a. -263KJ
b. 15.5 KJ
c. -15.5KJ
d. 263 KJ

26. The elements lithium, sodium, and potassium

a. are in the same period of elements.
b. are in the same group.
c. have the same mass number.
d. are isotopes of one another.

27. Place the following in the correct order of increasing acidity:

H_3PO_4, HF, HCl, H_2O, NH_3

a. $H_3PO4<H_2O<NH_3<HF<HCl$
b. $NH_3<H_2O<HF<H_3PO_4<HCl$
c. $H_2O<NH_3<HF<H_3PO_4<HCl$
d. $NH_3<H_2O<HF<HCl<H_3PO_4$

28. Which of the following substances contains a nonpolar covalent bond?

a. H_2O
b. N_2
c. NH_3
d. MgF_2

29. Which of the following types of chemicals are considered generally unsafe to store together?

I. Liquids and solids
II. Acids and bases
III. Reducing agents and oxidizing agents
IV. Metals and salts

a. I, II
b. II, III
c. III, IV
d. I, IV

30. Methane gas is burned in pure oxygen at 200 °C and 1 atm of pressure to produce CO_2 and H_2O according to the equation

$CH_4 + 2O_2 \rightarrow CO_2 + 2H_2O$

If 10 L of methane gas were burned, and the final temperature and pressure remained the same, how many liters of gaseous products are produced by the reaction?

Please provide your answer on the supplied griddable sheet.

31. How many milliliters of a 25% (m/v) sodium hydroxide (NaOH) solution would contain 75 grams of NaOH?

a. 19 ml
b. 75 ml
c. 33 ml
d. 3.0×10^2 ml

32. A 1 M solution of NaCl (A) and a 0.5 M solution of NaCl (B) are joined together by a semi permeable membrane. What, if anything, is likely to happen between the two solutions?

a. No change, the solvents and solutes are the same in each
b. Water will migrate from A to B
c. NaCl will migrate from A to B and water will migrate from B to A.
d. Water will migrate from B to A.

33. The carbon tetrachloride molecule (CCl_4) has the shape of a

a. cube.
b. sphere.
c. circle.
d. tetrahedron.

34. Which of the following is a physical change?

a. fermenting grapes to produce wine
b. dry ice subliming
c. baking a cake
d. digesting a meal

35. The _____ is the energy difference between reactants and products in a chemical reaction.

a. heat of reaction
b. transition energy
c. product energy
d. overall energy

36. The element in this list with chemical properties similar to magnesium is

a. carbon.
b. strontium.
c. chlorine.
d. boron.

37. What will be the pH of 2 L of a 0.1 M aqueous solution of HCl?

a. 2
b. -1
c. 1
d. 0.05

38. According to the Arrhenius concept, if HNO_3 were dissolved in water, it would act as

a. a base.
b. a proton acceptor.
c. a source of hydroxide ions.
d. an acid.

39. The density of a material refers to:

a. Mass per volume
b. Mass per mole
c. Molecular weight per volume
d. Moles per volume

40. A weather balloon is filled with 1000 mol of He gas at 25 °C and 101 kPa of pressure. What is the volume of the weather balloon?

Please provide your answer on the supplied griddable sheet.

41. In an atom, the nucleus contains

a. all the protons and electrons.
b. only protons.
c. an equal number of protons and electrons.
d. all the protons and neutrons.

42. According to the Brønsted-Lowry definition,

a. a base is a proton acceptor.
b. a base produces H^+ ions in aqueous solutions.
c. a base is a proton donor.
d. an acid is a proton acceptor.

43. The atomic number of an atom is equal to the number of

a. neutrons plus protons.
b. neutrons.
c. nuclei.
d. protons.

44. Which of the following is NOT a correct statement concerning gases?

a. The volume occupied by a gas is related to temperature and pressure.
b. A mole of a gas will occupy the same volume regardless of its molecular composition.
c. The change in volume due to changes in temperature is related to attractions among gas molecules.
d. If a gas is held in a constant volume and the pressure is increased, then the temperature will increase as well.

45. Which of the following gives the balanced equation for this reaction?

$K_3PO_4 + Ca(NO_3)_2 \rightarrow Ca_3(PO_4)_2 + KNO_3$

a. $K_3PO_4 + Ca(NO_3) + KNO_3$
b. $K_3PO_4 + Ca(NO_3)_2 \rightarrow Ca_3(PO_4)_2 + 3\ KNO_3$
c. $K_3PO_4 + Ca(NO_3)_2 \rightarrow Ca_3(PO_4)_2 + KNO_3$
d. $2\ K_3PO_4 + 3\ Ca(NO_3)_2 \rightarrow Ca_3(PO_4)_2 + 6\ KNO_3$

46. Which of the following is a characteristic of nonmetals?

a. good conductors of electricity
b. malleable
c. shiny
d. low melting points

47. 50 mL of 1 M H_2SO_4 is added to an aqueous solution containing 4 g of NaOH. What will the final pH of the resulting solution be?

a. 5
b. 6
c. 7
d. 9

48. Considering the following chemical equation, how many moles of oxygen gas are needed to react with 4 moles of magnesium (Mg)?

$2\ Mg + O_2 \rightarrow 2\ MgO$

a. 6.0 moles
b. 1.0 mole
c. 4.0 moles
d. 2.0 moles

49. The number of neutrons in an atom is equal to

a. the mass number.
b. the mass number minus the atomic number.
c. the mass number plus the atomic number.
d. the number of protons.

50. 100 mL of a 0.1 M solution of NaOH is neutralized to pH 7 with H_2SO_4. How many grams of H_2SO_4 are required to achieve this neutralization?

Please provide your answer on the supplied griddable sheet.

51. A chemical equation is balanced when

a. the charge on each atom is the same in reactants and products.
b. the total number of molecules is the same in reactants and products.
c. the sum of the coefficients of the reactants is equal to the sum of the coefficients of the products.
d. the number of atoms of each element is the same in reactants and products.

52. What would be the correct IUPAC name for the following compound?

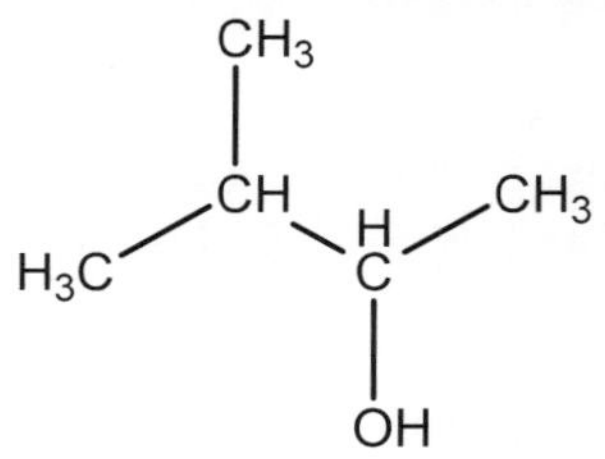

a. 3-methyl-2-butanol
b. 2-methyl-3-butanol
c. 3,3-dimethyl-2-propanol
d. 2-Hydroxy-3-methyl butane

Answers and Explanations

1. C: The freezing point of a solution is inversely correlated to the concentration of solute in the solution. Dividing the solution will have no impact on its properties. Driving off some of the solvent by heating will effectively increase the concentration and thus lower the freezing point. Precipitating out some of the solute will lower the concentration and increasing the freezing point.

2. A: The kinetic energy of the gas molecules is directly proportional to the temperature. If the temperature decreases, so does the molecular motion. A decrease in temperature will not necessarily mean a gas condenses to a liquid. Neither the mass nor the density is impacted, as no material was added or removed, and the volume remained the same.

3. B: Na (sodium) is a solid at standard temperature and pressure, which is $0^{\circ}C$ (273 K) and 100 kPa (0.986 atm), according to IUPAC. The stronger the intermolecular forces, the greater the likelihood of the material being a solid. Kr and Xe are noble gases and have negligible intermolecular attraction. NH_3 has some hydrogen bonding but is still a gas at STP. Sodium is an alkali metal whose atoms are bonded by metallic bonding and is therefore a solid at STP.

4. B: The dot structure shows all of the electrons in the outer, highest energy shell of an atom. It is a representation of the atom's valence, the number of electrons available for bond formation, and is not intended to show the location of these electrons or to convey any information as to the structure of the atom.

5. D: London dispersion forces are the weakest intermolecular forces. These interactions occur in all molecules due to unequal electron density around the nucleus, which results in a momentary dipole. Dipole-dipole interactions are those between two polar molecules. The more positive portion of one molecule is attracted to the negative portion of a different molecule. Hydrogen bonding is a stronger type of dipole-dipole interaction which occurs between a hydrogen in one molecule and a nitrogen, oxygen, or fluorine atom in another molecule. Hydrogen bonding only occurs between molecules containing H-F, H-O or H-N bonds. Ionic bonds are the strongest intermolecular forces. In ionic molecules, a positive ion is attracted to a negative ion. NaCl is entirely ionic with full charge separation, and the ions are tightly bound to each other in an organized crystalline network.

6. B: Ethane is an alkane and only very weakly acidic. Methanol, an alcohol, has a slightly acidic proton attached to the oxygen. Acetic acid is much more acidic than methanol with the acidic proton attached to the carboxyl group. Hydrochloric acid is highly acidic and completely dissociates in water.

7. C: Ionic bonds generally involve metals and nonmetals and involve one element losing its valence electrons to the other. In general, elements that are close together on the periodic table are more likely to share valence electrons and form covalent bonds.

8. D: To make a buffer, a weak acid and its conjugate base or a weak base and its conjugate acid are commonly used. Buffers work by using the common-ion effect and result in little change in the pH when an acid or a base is added. HCl/NaOH is a strong acid/strong base combination and will not result in a buffer solution. Although the $HNO_3/NaNO_3$ and $H_2SO_4/NaHSO_4$ mixtures are conjugate acid/base pairs, both HNO_3 and H_2SO_4 are strong acids, not weak acids. Neither of these solutions would result in a buffer. Only the NaH_2PO_4/Na_2HPO_4 mixture would result in a buffer as it is a combination of a weak acid and its conjugate base.

9. D: Since there are twice as many molecules of hydrogen present vs. oxygen, the partial pressure of hydrogen will be greater. The mass of hydrogen will not be greater than the mass of oxygen present even though there are more moles of hydrogen, due to oxygen having a higher molecular weight. Each gas will occupy the same volume. Hydrogen and oxygen gas can coexist in the container without reacting to produce water. There is no indication given that a chemical reaction has occurred.

10. C: The closer the data points are to each other, the more precise the data. This does not mean the data is accurate, but that the results are very reproducible.

11. B: The ionization energy is defined as the amount of energy necessary to remove the least tightly bound electron. It generally increases going across a period and decreases going down a group. For example, the ionization energy for lithium would actually be greater than that for potassium.

12. C: The O-H bond in water is a covalent bond. As electronegativity increases, going across the periodic chart from left to right, oxygen is considerably more electronegative than hydrogen and, as such, attracts the shared electrons more strongly than the hydrogen atoms, polarizing the negative charge toward the oxygen.

13. A: Since we have 1 liter of the solution, then 0.02 M represents 0.02 moles of methanol. The mass of methanol can then be found by 0.02mol x MW of CH_3OH (32) = 0.64 g. Molality is the moles of solute (methanol) divided by the number of kilograms of solvent; in this case, it is essentially 1 kg. This is assumed since the solvent is water and the density of water is 1 g/mL. So 0.02 mol/ 1 kg = 0.02 m.

14. A: When liquid water changes to steam, the temperature is constant, as in all phase changes. The entropy increases due to the increase in disorder from a liquid to a gas.

15. D: The periodic table is organized to group together, in the same column, elements which have similar chemical properties. By inspection, a review of the periodic table shows that transition elements are the "B" group elements, each period is a row representing a series of elements with increasing atomic numbers, and the representative elements include all the groups except the transition elements.

16. The balanced chemical equation given in this question shows that one mole of silver nitrate ($AgNO_3$) in the presence of sodium chloride (NaCl) will yield the same amount, one mole, of silver chloride (AgCl). We can calculate:

MW of $AgNO_3$ = (107.9) + 14.01 + (3 x 16.0) = 169.91

MW of AgCl = (107.9) + (35.5) = 143.4

100 g of $AgNO_3$ = 100 g/169.91 g per mole = 0.589 moles

0.589 mole x 143.4 g per mole = 84.4 grams

17. C: Three oxygen atoms are equal to a total charge of -6. Therefore, the two iron atoms must equal that with a positive charge, or +6. So each iron atom must be +3, and the compound is iron (III) oxide.

18. D: The octet rule can also be restated to say that all atoms gain and lose electrons to achieve a noble gas configuration, where the highest occupied energy level (electron shell) is fully occupied with eight, or a multiple of eight, electrons.

19. D: Electronegativity refers to the ability of an atom to attract bonding electrons. Nonpolarity, polarity, and ionic character refer to the charge distributions on atoms and molecules.

20. Using the decay formula, C-14 remaining = C-14 initial$(0.5)^{t/t\ half\text{-}life}$. So, 1 mg $(0.5)^{20000/5730}$ = 0.09 mg. This problem is best solved using the decay formula since 20,000 years is 3.5 half lives. If a student is careful in their reasoning, this problem can be solved without the decay formula. After 3 half-lives, there would be 0.125 mg remaining. If allowed to decay for 4 half-lives, 0.0625 mg would remain. Since only half of this half-life were allowed to elapse, only half of the material would decay, which would be 0.03 mg. Subtracting this amount from 0.125 mg, the amount remaining after 3 half-lives, gives 0.09 mg, which is the amount of material remaining after 3.5 half-lives.

21. A: Lewis acids are compounds capable of accepting a lone pair of electrons. $AlCl_3$ is a very strong Lewis acid and can readily accept a pair of electrons due to Al only having 6 electrons instead of 8 in its outer shell. $FeCl_3$ is also a strong Lewis acid, though milder than $AlCl_3$. Sulfuric acid is a Brønsted-Lowry acid since it produces protons. PCl_3 is a Lewis base since the P can donate its lone pair of electrons to another species.

22. C: Graham's law of diffusion allows one to calculate the relative diffusion rate between two different gases based on their masses.

23. D: Elements in Group IIA have two electrons in the highest energy level. For example, beryllium (Be), with an atomic number of 4, has two electrons in the first energy level and two in the second, leaving that shell only partially filled with room for six additional electrons. Similarly, magnesium (Mg) with an atomic number of 12 has the occupied energy levels containing two, eight, and two electrons. Again, the highest energy level is unfilled by six electrons. Therefore, to form an ion, the Group IIA elements lose two electrons, rather than gain six, to achieve a net charge of 2^+.

24. D: In a covalently bonded molecule, the number of electrons in the shared highest energy level is a noble gas arrangement.

25. C: Cooling means heat is leaving the system, so it must be negative. We have 5.9 mol of ammonia cooling 75 °C, or 75 K. So 5.9 mol x -75 K x 35.1 J/(mol)(K) = -15.5 kJ.

26. B: Lithium, sodium, and potassium are alkali metals (Group IA). They are neither in the same period (row) nor do they share a common mass or number of neutrons and, as such, are not isotopes of each other.

27. B: NH_3 is ammonia, which is a base. H_2O is amphoteric, meaning that it can act as either a weak acid or a weak base. HF is actually a weak acid, despite fluorine being the most electronegative atom. The small size of the F results in a stronger bond between the H and F, which reduces acidity since this bond will be harder to break. H_3PO_4, phosphoric acid, is high in acidity and HCl is a very strong acid, meaning it completely dissociates.

28. B: The polarity of a molecule refers to how equally electrons are shared between the atoms involved. In bonds involving compounds where there is no difference in the electronegativity between the atoms, the bond is nonpolar. Such is the case for N_2, a molecule of nitrogen where the two atoms are identical and, therefore, have the same electronegativity. In general, the partners in a covalent bond differ in electronegativity, causing the electrons not to be shared equally. Just bonds are termed polar, and the polarity is a function of the difference in electronegativity between the atoms.

29. B: Acids and bases will react violently if accidentally mixed, as will reducing and oxidizing agents. Both reactions can be highly exothermic and uncontrollable.

30. The equation shows that for every liter of methane reacted, one liter of CO_2 and 2 liters of water vapor will be produced. So a total of three liters of gaseous products will be formed for every liter of methane burned. Because the temperature of the reaction products is 200 °C, the water produced will be in vapor (gas) form and not in liquid form. Since 10L of methane were burned, 30 L of gaseous products were formed.

31. D: A 25% (m/v) NaOH solution contains, by definition, 25 grams of NaOH per 100 ml of total solution. Therefore, 300 ml of this solution would hold 75 grams of NaOH. [Calculate: 75 g/25 g = 3 x 100 = 300 = 3.0×10^2]

32. D: During osmosis, solvent flows from the lowest to the highest concentration of solute, in this case B to A. The membrane is semi-permeable and only allows the solvent to move, not the solute.

33. D: In carbon tetrachloride, four atoms of chlorine each share an electron with an atom of carbon. The interaction between each chlorine atom and the carbon molecule is identical, and the structure is symmetrical. It is a tetrahedron, where four chlorine atoms are spaced at equal distances from each other and surround the single carbon atom.

34. B: The sublimation of dry ice, that is the transition directly from a solid to a gas, represents a change in the physical state of carbon dioxide. No chemical bonds are broken or formed in the process. In contrast, fermentation (conversion of sugar to alcohol), baking, digestion of food, and a tomato ripening all involve one or more changes in the chemical composition of a complex mixture.

35. A: Reactions can be classified as to whether they yield (exothermic) or require energy (endothermic). The difference in energy in these cases is positive and negative, respectively, and is generally termed the heat of reaction. The transition and activation energies refer to the energy needed for specific molecular changes in the overall reaction.

36. B: Magnesium and strontium are both in group IIA of the periodic table. They are alkaline earth metals, which have similar chemical properties.

37. C: HCl is a strong acid that will completely dissociate. $pH = -\log_{10}[H^+]$, which for this problem is $pH=-\log_{10}(0.1) = 1$. The volume of the solution has no bearing on the pH since we know the concentration.

38. D: An Arrhenius acid is defined as a compound that when dissolved in water dissociates into a hydrogen ion (H^+) and a negatively charged ion, such as (NO_3^-). The compound HNO_3, nitric acid, is a proton donor and acid, which does not dissociate into a hydroxide (OH^-) when dissolved in water.

39. A: Density is mass per volume, typically expressed in units such as g/cm^3, or kg/m^3.

40. The ideal gas law PV=nRT is rearranged to solve for V, and we get V = nRT/P. R is the gas constant, 0.08206 L atm/mol K, and the Celsius temperature must be converted to Kelvin, by adding 273 to 25°C to obtain 298 K. The pressure must be converted to atmospheres, which 101 kPa is essentially 1 atm (0.9967 atm). Plugging the numbers into the equation we get V = 1000 mol

(0.08206 L atm/mol K)(298 K)/1 atm, which gives V = 24,453 L. A liter is a cubic decimeter (dm^3) and when converted gives V = 24.5 m^3.

41. D: The nucleus consists of neutrons and protons. While atoms generally have an equal number of electrons and protons, electrons are not a component of the nucleus.

42. A: The definition of a Brønsted-Lowry base is that it is a proton (H^+) acceptor, while acids are proton donors.

43. D: The atomic number of an element is defined as the number of protons found in the nucleus. This will be a constant for all the isotopes of an element, as well as for the ions formed from that element.

44. C: The equation of an Ideal Gas is as follows:

$$PV = nRT$$

where n corresponds to the moles of gas present. From this equation, one can determine how changes in temperature, pressure, and the volume occupied by a gas affect one another. The attraction among gas molecules is assumed to have negligible effects on the volume occupied by a gas.

45. D: Since atoms cannot be created or destroyed, under ordinary circumstances, a balanced chemical equation has the same number of each atom on both sides of the equation. Obviously, the first possibility (A) isn't an equation since only reactants are shown without any product. Equations B and C each have three atoms of calcium in the product, but only a single calcium atom in the reactants. Equation C also has only one atom of potassium in the product, while there are three potassium atoms in the reactants. Equation D is balanced since there are the same number of potassium (6), phosphorus (2), oxygen (20), calcium (3), and nitrogen (6) atoms on each side of the equation.

46. D: Nonmetals generally have relatively low melting points, are brittle, and are poor conductors of heat and electricity.

47. C: There are 0.05 mol of sulfuric acid being added, but a total of 0.10 mol of H^+ since sulfuric acid is diprotic (H_2SO_4). This is being added to 0.1 mol of NaOH. The moles of acid and base exactly cancel each other out; therefore the pH of the resulting aqueous solution will be near 7.

48. D: Oxygen gas exists as a diatomic molecule, O_2. Thus, in the balanced chemical equation given, two moles of magnesium are reacting with one mole of oxygen gas to form two moles of magnesium oxide (MgO). The formation of four moles of MgO would require twice as much oxygen, or 2.0 moles.

49. B: The atomic number of an element corresponds to the number of protons in the nucleus. The mass number is the number of protons plus the number of neutrons, i.e. the sum of the subatomic particles that have any appreciable mass.

50. 100 mL of a 0.1 M solution of NaOH contains 0.01 moles of NaOH. That means 0.01 moles of acid are required to completely neutralize the solution. The MW of sulfuric acid is 98, so 0.98 g of sulfuric acid is 0.01 mole. But since sulfuric acid has two equivalents of acid per mole, only 0.005 mole of the acid is required or 0.49 g.

51. D: The mass of reactants and products must be conserved, regardless of how atoms are rearranged to form new compounds. That this occurs for a particular equation can be established by ensuring that the same numbers of atoms of each element are represented on each side of the equation.

52. A: The longest straight chain of carbons is four, so the parent name is butane. The alcohol takes number precedence, so it is in the -2- position, placing the methyl in the -3- position. The suffix becomes –ol since it is an alcohol, so the name is 3-methyl-2-butanol.

Image Credits

Licensed Under CC BY-SA 3.0 (creativecommons.org/licenses/by-sa/3.0/deed.en)

Hydrogen Bonds: "3D model hydrogen bonds in water" by Wikimedia user Qwerter (https://commons.wikimedia.org/wiki/File:3D_model_hydrogen_bonds_in_water.svg)

How to Overcome Test Anxiety

Just the thought of taking a test is enough to make most people a little nervous. A test is an important event that can have a long-term impact on your future, so it's important to take it seriously and it's natural to feel anxious about performing well. But just because anxiety is normal, that doesn't mean that it's helpful in test taking, or that you should simply accept it as part of your life. Anxiety can have a variety of effects. These effects can be mild, like making you feel slightly nervous, or severe, like blocking your ability to focus or remember even a simple detail.

If you experience test anxiety—whether severe or mild—it's important to know how to beat it. To discover this, first you need to understand what causes test anxiety.

Causes of Test Anxiety

While we often think of anxiety as an uncontrollable emotional state, it can actually be caused by simple, practical things. One of the most common causes of test anxiety is that a person does not feel adequately prepared for their test. This feeling can be the result of many different issues such as poor study habits or lack of organization, but the most common culprit is time management. Starting to study too late, failing to organize your study time to cover all of the material, or being distracted while you study will mean that you're not well prepared for the test. This may lead to cramming the night before, which will cause you to be physically and mentally exhausted for the test. Poor time management also contributes to feelings of stress, fear, and hopelessness as you realize you are not well prepared but don't know what to do about it.

Other times, test anxiety is not related to your preparation for the test but comes from unresolved fear. This may be a past failure on a test, or poor performance on tests in general. It may come from comparing yourself to others who seem to be performing better or from the stress of living up to expectations. Anxiety may be driven by fears of the future—how failure on this test would affect your educational and career goals. These fears are often completely irrational, but they can still negatively impact your test performance.

Elements of Test Anxiety

As mentioned earlier, test anxiety is considered to be an emotional state, but it has physical and mental components as well. Sometimes you may not even realize that you are suffering from test anxiety until you notice the physical symptoms. These can include trembling hands, rapid heartbeat, sweating, nausea, and tense muscles. Extreme anxiety may lead to fainting or vomiting. Obviously, any of these symptoms can have a negative impact on testing. It is important to recognize them as soon as they begin to occur so that you can address the problem before it damages your performance.

The mental components of test anxiety include trouble focusing and inability to remember learned information. During a test, your mind is on high alert, which can help you recall information and stay focused for an extended period of time. However, anxiety interferes with your mind's natural processes, causing you to blank out, even on the questions you know well. The strain of testing during anxiety makes it difficult to stay focused, especially on a test that may take several hours. Extreme anxiety can take a huge mental toll, making it difficult not only to recall test information but even to understand the test questions or pull your thoughts together.

Effects of Test Anxiety

Test anxiety is like a disease—if left untreated, it will get progressively worse. Anxiety leads to poor performance, and this reinforces the feelings of fear and failure, which in turn lead to poor performances on subsequent tests. It can grow from a mild nervousness to a crippling condition. If allowed to progress, test anxiety can have a big impact on your schooling, and consequently on your future.

Test anxiety can spread to other parts of your life. Anxiety on tests can become anxiety in any stressful situation, and blanking on a test can turn into panicking in a job situation. But fortunately, you don't have to let anxiety rule your testing and determine your grades. There are a number of relatively simple steps you can take to move past anxiety and function normally on a test and in the rest of life.

Physical Steps for Beating Test Anxiety

While test anxiety is a serious problem, the good news is that it can be overcome. It doesn't have to control your ability to think and remember information. While it may take time, you can begin taking steps today to beat anxiety.

Just as your first hint that you may be struggling with anxiety comes from the physical symptoms, the first step to treating it is also physical. Rest is crucial for having a clear, strong mind. If you are tired, it is much easier to give in to anxiety. But if you establish good sleep habits, your body and mind will be ready to perform optimally, without the strain of exhaustion. Additionally, sleeping well helps you to retain information better, so you're more likely to recall the answers when you see the test questions.

Getting good sleep means more than going to bed on time. It's important to allow your brain time to relax. Take study breaks from time to time so it doesn't get overworked, and don't study right before bed. Take time to rest your mind before trying to rest your body, or you may find it difficult to fall asleep.

Along with sleep, other aspects of physical health are important in preparing for a test. Good nutrition is vital for good brain function. Sugary foods and drinks may give a burst of energy but this burst is followed by a crash, both physically and emotionally. Instead, fuel your body with protein and vitamin-rich foods.

Also, drink plenty of water. Dehydration can lead to headaches and exhaustion, especially if your brain is already under stress from the rigors of the test. Particularly if your test is a long one, drink water during the breaks. And if possible, take an energy-boosting snack to eat between sections.

Along with sleep and diet, a third important part of physical health is exercise. Maintaining a steady workout schedule is helpful, but even taking 5-minute study breaks to walk can help get your blood pumping faster and clear your head. Exercise also releases endorphins, which contribute to a positive feeling and can help combat test anxiety.

When you nurture your physical health, you are also contributing to your mental health. If your body is healthy, your mind is much more likely to be healthy as well. So take time to rest, nourish your body with healthy food and water, and get moving as much as possible. Taking these physical steps will make you stronger and more able to take the mental steps necessary to overcome test anxiety.

Mental Steps for Beating Test Anxiety

Working on the mental side of test anxiety can be more challenging, but as with the physical side, there are clear steps you can take to overcome it. As mentioned earlier, test anxiety often stems from lack of preparation, so the obvious solution is to prepare for the test. Effective studying may be the most important weapon you have for beating test anxiety, but you can and should employ several other mental tools to combat fear.

First, boost your confidence by reminding yourself of past success—tests or projects that you aced. If you're putting as much effort into preparing for this test as you did for those, there's no reason you should expect to fail here. Work hard to prepare; then trust your preparation.

Second, surround yourself with encouraging people. It can be helpful to find a study group, but be sure that the people you're around will encourage a positive attitude. If you spend time with others who are anxious or cynical, this will only contribute to your own anxiety. Look for others who are motivated to study hard from a desire to succeed, not from a fear of failure.

Third, reward yourself. A test is physically and mentally tiring, even without anxiety, and it can be helpful to have something to look forward to. Plan an activity following the test, regardless of the outcome, such as going to a movie or getting ice cream.

When you are taking the test, if you find yourself beginning to feel anxious, remind yourself that you know the material. Visualize successfully completing the test. Then take a few deep, relaxing breaths and return to it. Work through the questions carefully but with confidence, knowing that you are capable of succeeding.

Developing a healthy mental approach to test taking will also aid in other areas of life. Test anxiety affects more than just the actual test—it can be damaging to your mental health and even contribute to depression. It's important to beat test anxiety before it becomes a problem for more than testing.

Study Strategy

Being prepared for the test is necessary to combat anxiety, but what does being prepared look like? You may study for hours on end and still not feel prepared. What you need is a strategy for test prep. The next few pages outline our recommended steps to help you plan out and conquer the challenge of preparation.

Step 1: Scope Out the Test

Learn everything you can about the format (multiple choice, essay, etc.) and what will be on the test. Gather any study materials, course outlines, or sample exams that may be available. Not only will this help you to prepare, but knowing what to expect can help to alleviate test anxiety.

Step 2: Map Out the Material

Look through the textbook or study guide and make note of how many chapters or sections it has. Then divide these over the time you have. For example, if a book has 15 chapters and you have five days to study, you need to cover three chapters each day. Even better, if you have the time, leave an extra day at the end for overall review after you have gone through the material in depth.

If time is limited, you may need to prioritize the material. Look through it and make note of which sections you think you already have a good grasp on, and which need review. While you are studying, skim quickly through the familiar sections and take more time on the challenging parts.

Write out your plan so you don't get lost as you go. Having a written plan also helps you feel more in control of the study, so anxiety is less likely to arise from feeling overwhelmed at the amount to cover.

Step 3: Gather Your Tools

Decide what study method works best for you. Do you prefer to highlight in the book as you study and then go back over the highlighted portions? Or do you type out notes of the important information? Or is it helpful to make flashcards that you can carry with you? Assemble the pens, index cards, highlighters, post-it notes, and any other materials you may need so you won't be distracted by getting up to find things while you study.

If you're having a hard time retaining the information or organizing your notes, experiment with different methods. For example, try color-coding by subject with colored pens, highlighters, or post-it notes. If you learn better by hearing, try recording yourself reading your notes so you can listen while in the car, working out, or simply sitting at your desk. Ask a friend to quiz you from your flashcards, or try teaching someone the material to solidify it in your mind.

Step 4: Create Your Environment

It's important to avoid distractions while you study. This includes both the obvious distractions like visitors and the subtle distractions like an uncomfortable chair (or a too-comfortable couch that makes you want to fall asleep). Set up the best study environment possible: good lighting and a comfortable work area. If background music helps you focus, you may want to turn it on, but otherwise keep the room quiet. If you are using a computer to take notes, be sure you don't have any other windows open, especially applications like social media, games, or anything else that could distract you. Silence your phone and turn off notifications. Be sure to keep water close by so you stay hydrated while you study (but avoid unhealthy drinks and snacks).

Also, take into account the best time of day to study. Are you freshest first thing in the morning? Try to set aside some time then to work through the material. Is your mind clearer in the afternoon or evening? Schedule your study session then. Another method is to study at the same time of day that you will take the test, so that your brain gets used to working on the material at that time and will be ready to focus at test time.

Step 5: Study!

Once you have done all the study preparation, it's time to settle into the actual studying. Sit down, take a few moments to settle your mind so you can focus, and begin to follow your study plan. Don't give in to distractions or let yourself procrastinate. This is your time to prepare so you'll be ready to fearlessly approach the test. Make the most of the time and stay focused.

Of course, you don't want to burn out. If you study too long you may find that you're not retaining the information very well. Take regular study breaks. For example, taking five minutes out of every hour to walk briskly, breathing deeply and swinging your arms, can help your mind stay fresh.

As you get to the end of each chapter or section, it's a good idea to do a quick review. Remind yourself of what you learned and work on any difficult parts. When you feel that you've mastered the material, move on to the next part. At the end of your study session, briefly skim through your notes again.

But while review is helpful, cramming last minute is NOT. If at all possible, work ahead so that you won't need to fit all your study into the last day. Cramming overloads your brain with more information than it can process and retain, and your tired mind may struggle to recall even previously learned information when it is overwhelmed with last-minute study. Also, the urgent nature of cramming and the stress placed on your brain contribute to anxiety. You'll be more likely to go to the test feeling unprepared and having trouble thinking clearly.

So don't cram, and don't stay up late before the test, even just to review your notes at a leisurely pace. Your brain needs rest more than it needs to go over the information again. In fact, plan to finish your studies by noon or early afternoon the day before the test. Give your brain the rest of the day to relax or focus on other things, and get a good night's sleep. Then you will be fresh for the test and better able to recall what you've studied.

Step 6: Take a Practice Test

Many courses offer sample tests, either online or in the study materials. This is an excellent resource to check whether you have mastered the material, as well as to prepare for the test format and environment.

Check the test format ahead of time: the number of questions, the type (multiple choice, free response, etc.), and the time limit. Then create a plan for working through them. For example, if you have 30 minutes to take a 60-question test, your limit is 30 seconds per question. Spend less time on the questions you know well so that you can take more time on the difficult ones.

If you have time to take several practice tests, take the first one open book, with no time limit. Work through the questions at your own pace and make sure you fully understand them. Gradually work up to taking a test under test conditions: sit at a desk with all study materials put away and set a timer. Pace yourself to make sure you finish the test with time to spare and go back to check your answers if you have time.

After each test, check your answers. On the questions you missed, be sure you understand why you missed them. Did you misread the question (tests can use tricky wording)? Did you forget the information? Or was it something you hadn't learned? Go back and study any shaky areas that the practice tests reveal.

Taking these tests not only helps with your grade, but also aids in combating test anxiety. If you're already used to the test conditions, you're less likely to worry about it, and working through tests until you're scoring well gives you a confidence boost. Go through the practice tests until you feel comfortable, and then you can go into the test knowing that you're ready for it.

Test Tips

On test day, you should be confident, knowing that you've prepared well and are ready to answer the questions. But aside from preparation, there are several test day strategies you can employ to maximize your performance.

First, as stated before, get a good night's sleep the night before the test (and for several nights before that, if possible). Go into the test with a fresh, alert mind rather than staying up late to study.

Try not to change too much about your normal routine on the day of the test. It's important to eat a nutritious breakfast, but if you normally don't eat breakfast at all, consider eating just a protein bar. If you're a coffee drinker, go ahead and have your normal coffee. Just make sure you time it so that the caffeine doesn't wear off right in the middle of your test. Avoid sugary beverages, and drink enough water to stay hydrated but not so much that you need a restroom break 10 minutes into the test. If your test isn't first thing in the morning, consider going for a walk or doing a light workout before the test to get your blood flowing.

Allow yourself enough time to get ready, and leave for the test with plenty of time to spare so you won't have the anxiety of scrambling to arrive in time. Another reason to be early is to select a good seat. It's helpful to sit away from doors and windows, which can be distracting. Find a good seat, get out your supplies, and settle your mind before the test begins.

When the test begins, start by going over the instructions carefully, even if you already know what to expect. Make sure you avoid any careless mistakes by following the directions.

Then begin working through the questions, pacing yourself as you've practiced. If you're not sure on an answer, don't spend too much time on it, and don't let it shake your confidence. Either skip it and come back later, or eliminate as many wrong answers as possible and guess among the remaining ones. Don't dwell on these questions as you continue—put them out of your mind and focus on what lies ahead.

Be sure to read all of the answer choices, even if you're sure the first one is the right answer. Sometimes you'll find a better one if you keep reading. But don't second-guess yourself if you do immediately know the answer. Your gut instinct is usually right. Don't let test anxiety rob you of the information you know.

If you have time at the end of the test (and if the test format allows), go back and review your answers. Be cautious about changing any, since your first instinct tends to be correct, but make sure you didn't misread any of the questions or accidentally mark the wrong answer choice. Look over any you skipped and make an educated guess.

At the end, leave the test feeling confident. You've done your best, so don't waste time worrying about your performance or wishing you could change anything. Instead, celebrate the successful completion of this test. And finally, use this test to learn how to deal with anxiety even better next time.

Review Video: Test Anxiety
Visit mometrix.com/academy and enter code: 100340

Important Qualification

Not all anxiety is created equal. If your test anxiety is causing major issues in your life beyond the classroom or testing center, or if you are experiencing troubling physical symptoms related to your anxiety, it may be a sign of a serious physiological or psychological condition. If this sounds like your situation, we strongly encourage you to seek professional help.

Thank You

We at Mometrix would like to extend our heartfelt thanks to you, our friend and patron, for allowing us to play a part in your journey. It is a privilege to serve people from all walks of life who are unified in their commitment to building the best future they can for themselves.

The preparation you devote to these important testing milestones may be the most valuable educational opportunity you have for making a real difference in your life. We encourage you to put your heart into it—that feeling of succeeding, overcoming, and yes, conquering will be well worth the hours you've invested.

We want to hear your story, your struggles and your successes, and if you see any opportunities for us to improve our materials so we can help others even more effectively in the future, please share that with us as well. **The team at Mometrix would be absolutely thrilled to hear from you!** So please, send us an email (support@mometrix.com) and let's stay in touch.

If you'd like some additional help, check out these other resources we offer for your exam:
http://MometrixFlashcards.com/SOL

Online Resources

Due to our efforts to try to keep this book to a manageable length, we've created a link that will give you access to all of your online resources:

mometrix.com/resources719/vsolchem

It's Your Moment, Let's Celebrate It!

Share your story @mometrixtestpreparation